Joseph P. Holbrook

Quartet and Chorus Choir Companion to Songs for the Sanctuary

Joseph P. Holbrook

Quartet and Chorus Choir Companion to Songs for the Sanctuary

ISBN/EAN: 9783337296735

Printed in Europe, USA, Canada, Australia, Japan

Cover: Foto ©Thomas Meinert / pixelio.de

More available books at **www.hansebooks.com**

QUARTET AND CHORUS

CHOIR.

~~~~◆►~~~~

COMPANION TO

SONGS FOR THE SANCTUARY,

By JOSEPH P. HOLBROOK,

Director of Music in the First Presbyterian Church,

BROOKLYN, N. Y.

~~~~◆►~~~~

NEW YORK:

Published by A. S. BARNES & CO.,

111 & 113 William Street.

1871.

QUARTET AND CHORUS CHOIR.

Hymn 743. **DUFFIELD. L. M.** Oberthür.

1. None loves me, Sav - iour, with thy love, ... None else can meet such needs as mine, as mine;
2. Give me a faith shall nev - er fail,.... One that shall al - ways work by love, by love;

3. A heart, that, when my days are glad,..... May nev - er from thy way de - cline, decline,

Oh! grant me, as thou shalt ap - prove. All that be - fits a child of thine!....
And then, what-ev - er foes as - sail, They shall but high - er cour - age move....

And when the sky of life grows sad, May still sub - mit its will to thine,—

From ev - ery fear and doubt re - lease, And give me con - fi - dence and peace.
More bold-ly for the truth to strive, And more by faith in thee to live:--

A heart that loves to trust in thee, A patient heart, cre - ate in me!

Hymns 8 & 147.   EELLS.   L. M.   J. P. H.

1. An-oth-er six days' work is done, An-oth-er Sab-bath is be-gun;

3. This heavenly calm, with-in the breast, Is the dear pledge of glo-rious rest,

Re-turn, my soul! en-joy thy rest, Im-prove the day thy God has blessed.

Which for the church of God re-mains— The end of cares, the end of pains.

2. Oh, that our thoughts and thanks may rise, As grate-ful in-cense to the skies;

4. In ho-ly du-ties, let the day, In ho-ly pleas-ures, pass a-way;

And draw, from heaven, that sweet re-pose, Which none, but he that feels it, knows.

How sweet a Sab-bath thus to spend. In hope of one that ne'er shall end.

Hymn 2. **SPOHR.** **L. M.** Spohr.

1. Thine earth - ly Sab - baths, Lord, we love, But there's a no - bler rest a - bove;

2. No more fa - tigue, no more dis-tress, Nor sin nor death shall reach the place;

To that our long-ing souls as - pire, With cheer - ful hope and strong de - sire.

No groans shall min - gle with the songs That war - ble from im - mor - tal tongues.

Hymn 6. **BRAYTON.** **L. M.** Methfessel.

1. Sweet is the work, my God! my King! To praise thy name, give thanks and sing:

2. Sweet is the day of sa - cred rest. No mor - tal care shall seize my breast:

To show thy love by morn-ing light. And talk of all thy truth at night.

Oh! may my heart in tune be found, Like Da - vid's harp of sol - emn sound.

Hymn 631. **AUSTEN. L. M.** Donizetti.

1. My God, per-mit me not to be · A stranger to my-self and thee;

2. Why should my pas-sions mix with earth, And thus de-base my heavenly birth?

A - mid a thousand thoughts I rove, For-get-ful of my high-est love.

Why should I cleave to things be - low, And let my God, my Sa-viour go?

Hymn 563. **BARTLETT. L. M.** J. P. H.

1. For-give us, Lord! to thee we cry, For-give us through thy matchless grace.

2. For-give thou us, as we for-give The ills we suf-fer from our foes;

On thee a-lone our souls re - ly, Be thou our strength and right-eous-ness.

Re-store us Lord! and bid us live: Oh! let us in thine arms re-pose.

Hymn 624. PATTON. L. M. J. P. H.

SOPRANO SOLO.

1. Re - turn, my rov - ing heart, re - turn, And life's vain shad - ows, chase no more;
3. Thro' all the wind - ings of my heart, My search let heaven - ly wis - dom guide;

Seek out some sol - i - tude to mourn, And thy for - sak - en God im -
And still its beams un - err - ing dart, Till all be known and pu - ri -

TRIO. p cres.

2. O thou great God! whose piercing eye, Dis - tinct - ly marks each deep re - treat;

plore. }
fied. }
4. Then let the vis - its of thy love, My in - most soul be made to share,

In these se - questered hours draw nigh, And let me here thy pre - sence meet.

Till ev - ery grace com - bine to prove, That God has fixed his dwell - ing there.

Hymn 256. **HUTCHINSON. L. M.** Schubert.

1. Blest Trin-i-ty! from mor-tal sight, Vailed in thine own e-ter-nal light!

3. The Fa-ther is in 'God the Son, And with the Fa-ther he..... is...... one;.....

We thee con-fess, in thee be-lieve; To thee with lov-ing hearts we cleave.

In both the Spir-it doth a-bide, And with them both is glo-ri-fied.

2. O Fa-ther! thou Most Ho-ly One! O God of God! E-ter-nal Son!

4. E-ter-nal Fa-ther! thee we praise! To thee, O Son! our hymns we raise;

O Ho-ly Ghost! thou Love Di-vine! To join them both is ev-er thine.

O Ho-ly Ghost! we thee a-dore. One mighty God for ev-er-more.

Hymn 470. KING. L. M. Arr.

Andante.

1. In - fi - nite Love! what pre - cious stores Thy mer - cy has pre - pared for us!

3. How rich the grace! the gift how free! 'Tis on - ly ask — it shall be given;

The cost - liest gems, the rich - est ores Could nev - er have en - dowed us thus.

'Tis on - ly knock, and thou shalt see The open - ing door that leads to heaven.

rit.

2. But thy soft hand, O gra - cious Lord! Can draw from suff - 'ring souls the sting:

4. Oh! then a - rise and take the good So full and free - ly prof - fer'd thee,

And thy rich boun - ty to our board Can bread for hung - 'ring sin - ners bring,

Re - membering that it cost the blood Of Him who died on Cal - va - ry.

Hymn 635.   **ROCKWELL. L. M.**   J. P. H.

1. God of my life! through all my days My grate - ful powers shall sound thy praise;

Duet.
3. When death o'er na - ture shall pre - vail, And all my powers of lan - guage fail.

The song shall wake with open - ing light, And war - ble to the si - lent night.

Joy through my swim - ming eyes shall break, And mean the thanks I can - not speak.

2. When anx - ious care would break my rest, And grief would tear my throb - bing breast,

Duet.
4. But, oh! when that last con - flict's o'er, And I am chained to flesh no more,

Thy tune - ful prais - es raised on high, Shall check the mur - mur and the sigh.

With what glad ac - cents shall I rise To join the mu - sic of the skies!

Hymn 626.　　ERIE.　L. M.　　Arranged.

1. When, gracious Lord, when shall it be That I shall find my all.... in thee—

3. Lord, I am blind—be thou my sight; Lord, I am weak—be thou my might;

The full-ness of thy prom - ise prove, The seal of thine e - ter - nal love?

A help - er of the help - less be; And let me find my all..... in thee.

Hymn 622.　　FISHER.　L. M.　　J. P. H.

1. Je - sus demands this heart of mine, Demands my love, my joy, my care;

2. 'Tis sin, a - las! with dread-ful power, Di - vides my Sav - iour from my sight;

But ah! how dead to things di - vine, How cold my best af - fec - tions are!

Oh, for one hap - py, cloud - less hour Of sa-cred free - dom, sweet de - light!

Hymn 381.   SHELDON.   L. M.

LYSBERG, arr. by D. R. STANFORD.

1. Go, wor-ship at Im-man-uel's feet: See in his face what won-ders meet:

Earth is too nar-row to ex-press His worth, his glo-ry, or his grace.

2. Nor earth, nor seas, nor sun, nor stars, Nor heav'n his full re-sem-blance bears:

His beau-ties we can nev-er trace, Till we be-hold him face to face.

SHELDON. Concluded.

3. Oh, let me climb those high - er skies, Where storms and dark - ness nev - er rise:

There he dis - plays his pow'r a - broad, And shines, and reigns, th'in - car - nate God.

Hymn 626. **LYON. L. M.** SPOHR.

Grazioso.

1. When, gra - cious Lord, when shall it be That I shall find my all in thee—

2. Ah! where-fore did I ev - er doubt? Thou wilt in no wise cast me out—

The full - ness of thy prom - ise prove, The seal of thine e - ter - nal love?

A help - less soul that comes to thee With on - ly sin and mis - e - ry.

Hymn 870.

(Songs of the Church)

WYMAN. L. M.

Weber, arr. by D. R. Stanford

1. When, as re-turns this sol-emn day,... Man comes to meet his Mak-er, God,

3. Vain, sin-ful man! cre-a-tion's Lord... Thy gold-en off-'rings well may spare;

What rites, what hon-ors shall he pay? How spread his sov-'reign name.. a-broad?

But give thy heart, and thou shalt find Here dwells a God who hear-eth prayer.

2. From mar-ble domes and gild-ed spires Shall curl-ing clouds of in-cense rise,...

4. Oh, grant us, in this sol-emn hour, From earth and sin's al-lurements free,...

And gems, and gold, and gar-lands deck The cost-ly pomp of sac-ri-fice!

To feel thy love, to own thy power, And raise each rap-tured thought to thee!

WYMAN. Concluded.

And gems, and gold, and gar - lands deck The cost-ly pomp of sac - ri - fice?....

To feel thy love, to own thy power, And raise each rap - tured thought to thee!....

Hymn 565. **FRENCH. L. M. 6l.** J. P. H.

1. "Per - fect in love!" Lord, can it be, A - mid this state of doubt and sin?

2. O Lord! a - mid this men - tal night, A - mid the clouds of dark dis - may,

While foes so thick with - out, I see, With weak - ness, pain, dis - ease with - in:

A - rise! A - rise! shed forth thy light, And kin - dle love's me - rid - ian day:

Can per - fect love in - hab - it here, And strong in faith, ex - tin - guish fear?

My Sav - iour God, to me ap - pear, So love shall tri - umph ov - er fear.

Hymn 990.   **HANDY.   L. M. 6l.**   J. P. H.

1. At even-ing time let there be light; Life's lit-tle day draws near its close:

2. At even-ing time let there be light; Storm-y and dark hath been my day;

A - round me fall the shades of night, The night of death, the grave's re - pose;

Yet rose the morn di - vine - ly bright; Dews, birds, and blos - soms cheered the way;

To crown my joys, to end my woes, At even - ing time let there be light.

Oh, for one sweet, one part - ing ray! At even - ing time let there be light.

Hymn 744.   **WOODHULL.   L. M. 6l.**   J. P. H.

1. My Sav - iour, thou thy love to me, In want, in pain, in shame, hast shown,

2. Oh, that I, like a lit - tle child, May fol - low thee; nor ev - er rest

WOODHULL. Concluded.

For me up - on th' ac - curs - ed tree, Didst by thy pre - cious death a - tone;

Till sweet - ly thou hast poured thy mild And low - ly mind in - to my breast!

. Thy death up - on my heart im - press, That noth - ing may it thence e - rase.

Oh, may I now and ev - er be, One spir - it, dear - est Lord, with thee!

Hymn 693. **DWIGHT. L. M.** Bellini.

1. O Love Di - vine! that stooped to share Our sharp - est pang, our bit - terest tear,

2. Tho' long the wea - ry way we tread, And sor - row crown each lin - gering year,

On thee we cast each earth - born care, We smile at pain while Thou art near.

No path we shun, no dark - ness dread, Our hearts still whis - pering, Thou art near.

Hymn 469.   HAYES.   L. M.   Rossini.

1. Would you see Je - sus? come with prayer, And heart re - pent - ant, to his feet;

3. Would you see Je - sus? day by day Let thought and con - verse be on high,

None who will right - ly seek him there, Shall fail his face of.... love to greet.

rit. piu.   *Fine.*

And hastening on the heavenward way, With Je - sus live, with.. Je - sus die.

Solo.

2. Would you see Je - sus? come.. with faith, And search the word his grace hath given,........

rit.   *tempo.*

For help and guid - ance in.... the path, That leads to his a - bode in heaven.

D. C.

Hymn 622. BOOTH. L. M. Ernst Jonas.

1. Je - sus de - mands this heart of mine, De - mands my love, my joy, my care;

3. Come, gra - cious Lord! thy love can raise My cap - tive powers from sin and death.

But ah! how dead to things di - vine, How cold my best af - fec - tions are!

And fill my heart and life with praise, And tune my last ex - pir - ing breath.

Contralto Solo.

2. 'Tis sin, a - las! with dread - ful power, Di - vides my Sav - iour from my sight;

Oh, for one hap - py, cloud - less hour Of sa - cred free - dom, sweet de - light!

Hymn 449.   STEELE.   L. M.   CONCONE.

1. Now to the power of God su - preme Be ev - er - last - ing hon - ors given;

3. 'Twas his own pur - pose that be - gan To res - cue reb - els doomed to die:

He saves from hell,— we bless his name,— He guides our wan - dering feet to heaven.

He gave us grace in Christ, his Son, Be - fore he spread the star - ry sky.

2. Not for our du - ties or de - serts, But of his own a - bound - ing grace,

4. Je - sus, the Lord, ap - pears at last, And makes his Fa - ther's coun - sels known;

He works sal - va - tion in our hearts, And forms a peo - ple for his praise.

De - clares the great trans - ac - tion past, And brings im - mor - tal bless - ings down.

Hymn 693. **RHODES. L. M.** J. P. H.

1. O Love Di - vine! that stooped to share Our sharp - est pang, our bit - t'rest tear,

2. Though long the wea - ry way we tread, And sor - row crown each lin - g'ring year,

On thee we cast each earth - born care, We smile at pain while Thou art near.

No path we shun, no dark - ness dread, Our hearts still whispering, Thou art near.

Hymn 985. **WHIPPLE. L. M.** J. P. H.

1. Je - sus! our best be - lov - ed Friend, On thy re - deem - ing name we call;

2. Our souls and bod - ies we re - sign, To fear and fol - low thy com - mands;

Je - sus! in love to us de - scend, Par - don and sanc - ti - fy us all.

Oh! take our hearts, our hearts are thine, Ac - cept the ser - vice of our hands.

Hymn 632.　　　　ELLIOTT. L. M.　　　　Rodwell.

Duet. Soprano and Tenor.

1. From deep dis - tress and troub - led thoughts, To thee, my God, I raise my cries;

3. My trust is fix'd up - on thy word, Nor shall I trust thy word in vain;

Quartet.

If thou se - vere - ly mark our faults, No flesh can stand be - fore thine eyes.

Let mourning souls ad - dress the Lord, And find re - lief from all their pain.

Chorus.

2. But thou hast built thy throne of grace, Free to dis - pense thy par - dons there,

4. Great is his love and large his grace, Through the re - demp - tion of his Son;

Quartet.

But thou hast built thy throne of grace, Free to dis - pense thy par - dons there.

Great is his love, and large his grace, Through the re - demp - tion of his Son;

ELLIOTT. Concluded.

That sin - ners may.... ap - proach thy face, And hope and

He turns our feet..... from sin - ful ways, And par - dons

love, and hope and love,.. And hope and love,.. as well as fear.

what our hands have done,.. And par - dons what.. our hands have done.

Hymn 259. **RIPLEY. L. M.** J. P. H.

1. There is a God!—all na - ture speaks, Thro' earth, and air, and seas, and skies;

2. The ris - ing sun, se - rene - ly bright, O'er the wide world's ex - tend - ed frame,

See! from the clouds his glo - ry breaks, When the first beams of morn - ing rise.

In - scribes, in char - ac - ters of light, His might - y Mak - er's glo - rious name.

Hymn 788. **RICHARDS. L. M.** J. P H.

1. Though sorrows rise and dan - gers roll, In waves of dark - ness o'er my soul;

2. Though Sinai's curse, in thun - der dread, Peals o'er mine un - pro - tect - ed head.

Though friends are false, and love de - cays, And few and e - vil are my days;
mp *f cres.*

And memory points, with bus - y pain. To grace and mer - cy given in vain;

Though conscience, fierc - est of my foes, Swells with re - mem - bered guilt my woes;
f

Till nature, shrink - ing in the strife, Would fly to hell to 'scape from life;

Yet ev'n in na - ture's ut - most ill, I love thee, Lord! I love thee still!
pp *ff* *pp* *rit.*

Though ev - ery thought has power to kill, I love thee, Lord! I love thee still!

Hymn 742.   BACON.   L. M. 6l.

Moderato.

1. When, stream-ing from the east-ern skies, The morn-ing light sa-lutes mine eyes,

2. And when to heaven's all-glo-rious King My morn-ing sac-ri-fice I bring,

O Sun of right-eous-ness di-vine, On me with beams of mer-cy shine!

And, mourn-ing o'er my guilt and shame, Ask mer-cy in my Sav-iour's name;

Oh! chase the clouds of guilt a-way, And turn my dark-ness in-to day,

Then, Je-sus, cleanse me with thy blood, And be my Ad-vo-cate with God,

And turn my dark-ness in-to.... day.

And be my Ad-vo-cate with God.

3.
When each day's scenes and labors close,
And wearied nature seeks repose,
With pardoning mercy richly blest,
Guard me, my Saviour, while I rest;
And, as each morning sun shall rise,
Oh, lead me onward to the skies!

Hymn 83.　　　　　MAIRAN. L. M.　　　　Arranged.

1. Blest hour! when mortal man re - tires...... To hold commun - ion with his God,
3. Blest hour! when God him-self draws nigh,..... Well pleased his peo - ple's voice to hear,

To send to heaven his warm de - sires,..... And list-en to the sa - cred word....
To hush the pen - i - ten - tial sigh, ... And wipe a - way the mourn-er's tear,.....

2. Blest hour! when earth-ly cares re - sign　Their em - pire o'er his anx - ious breast,....

4. Blest hour! for where the Lord re - sorts—　Foretastes of fu - ture bliss are given;....

While all a-round the calm di - vine　Proclaims the ho - ly day of rest.

And mor-tals find his earth-ly courts　The house of God, the gate of Heaven!

DUET.—BASS & CONTRALTO.

1. Like morning, when her ear - ly breeze Breaks up the sur - face of the seas,

3 Till Da - vid touched his sa - cred lyre, In si - lence lay th'un - breath - ing wire;

That, in their fur - rows dark with night, Her hand may sow the seeds of light,—

But when he swept its chords a - long, The an - gels stooped to hear the song.

DUET.—BASS & CONTRALTO.

2. Thy grace can send its breath - ings o'er The spir - it dark and lost be - fore;

4. So sleeps the soul, till thou, O Lord, Shalt deign to touch its life - less chord;

And, fresh'ning all its depths, pre - pare For truth di - vine to en - - ter there.

Till, waked by thee, its breath shall rise In mu - sic wor - thy of the skies.

Hymn 469.   BELKNAP.   L. M.   Novello.

Larghetto.
SOPRANO SOLO.

1, Would you see Je - sus? come with prayer And heart re - pent - ant to his feet;

pp

DUET.—SOPRANO & CONTRALTO.

None who will right - ly seek him there, Shall fail his face of love to greet.

pp

2, Would you see Je - sus? come with faith, And search the word his grace hath given,

2, Would you see Je - sus? come with faith, And search the word his grace hath given,

For help and guid - ance in the path That leads to his a - bode in heaven.

For help and guid - ance in the path That leads to his a - bode in heaven.

BELKNAP. Concluded.

3, Would you see Je - sus? day by day   Let thought and con - verse be on high,....

Duet.

3. Would you see Je - sus? day by day   Let thought and con - verse be on high,....

And hastening on the heavenward way,   With Je - sus live, with Je - sus die.

And hastening on the heavenward way,   With Je - sus live, with Je - sus die.

Hymn 568.   **BLAKE. L. M.**   J. P. H.

1. Thou on - ly Sov - ereign of my heart,   My Ref - uge, my al - might - y Friend—

2. Whith-er, ah ! whith- er shall I go,   A wretch - ed wan - d'rer from my Lord ?

And can my soul from thee de - part,   On whom a - lone my hopes de-pend !

Can this dark world of sin and woe   One glimpse of hap - pi - ness af-ford ?

Hymn 287.　　　　　DANNER. L. M.　　　　Lentz.

1. When, marshaled on the night-ly plain, The glitt'ring host be - stud the sky,

3. Once on the rag - ing seas I rode, The storm was loud, the night was dark,—

One star a - lone, of all the train, Can fix the sin - ner's wand - 'ring eye.

The o - cean yawned—and rude-ly blowed The wind, that tossed my found - 'ring bark.

2. Hark! hark! to God...................... the cho - rus breaks, From ev - ery
4. Deep hor - ror then...................... my vi - tals froze, Death-struck, I

Hark! hark! to God the cho - rus breaks,
Deep hor - ror then my vi - tals froze,

host,.............. from ev - - ery gem; But one a - lone the Sav-iour speaks,—
ceased............

From ev - ery host,
Death-struck, I ceased the tide.... to stem;— When sud - den-ly a star a - rose,—

DANNER. Concluded.

It is the Star of Beth - le - hem, It is the Star of Beth - le - hem.

It was the Star of Beth - le - hem, It was the Star of Beth - le - hem.

Hymn 556. SUMNER. L. M. 6 lines. LYSBERG.

1. Wea - ry of wandering from my God, And now made will - ing to re - turn,

2. O Je - sus, full of truth and grace,— More full of grace than I of sin;

I hear, and bow me to the rod: Yet not in hopeless grief I mourn;

Yet once a - gain I seek thy face, O - pen thine arms, and take me in!

I have an ad - vo - cate a - bove, A friend be - fore the throne of love.

And free - ly my back - slid - ings heal, And love thy faith - less ser - vant still.

Hymn 379.　　　　　HAMMOND.　L. M.　　　　　J. P. H.

1. The King of saints,—how fair his face! A - dorned with maj - es - ty and grace,

3. Oh! hap - py hour, when thou shalt rise To his fair pal - ace in the skies;

He comes, with blessings from a - bove, And wins the na - tions to his love.

And all thy sons, a numerous train, Each, like a prince, in glo - ry reign.

2. At his right hand, our eyes be - hold The queen, ar - rayed in pur - est gold;

4. Let end - less hon - ors crown his head: Let ev - ery age his prais - es spread;

The world ad - mires her heaven - ly dress, Her robe of joy and right - eous - ness.

While we, with cheer - ful songs, ap - prove The con - de - scen - sion of his love.

Hymn 188. **LEWIS. L. M.** Arranged.

1. O God, the Light of all that live, Unmoved, who dost all mo-tion sway, The times and seasons

2. At ev-en-tide let there be light; So may our souls no sun-set see, And death to us the

who dost give, And thro' its chang-es guide the day ! And thro' its chang-es guide the day !

por-tal bright To an e-ter-nal morn-ing be, To an e-ter-nal morn-ing be.

Hymn 195. **BENTON. L. M.** W. H. Monk.

1. 'Twas by an or-der from the Lord The an-cient proph-ets spoke his word;

2. The works and won-ders which they wrought Con-firmed the mes-sa-ges they brought;

'His Spir-it did their tongues in-spire, And warmed their hearts with heavenly fire.

The prophet's pen suc-ceeds his breath, To save the ho-ly words from death.

Hymn 449.   **TALBERT. L. M.**   J. P. H.

DUET.—BASS & CONTRALTO.

1. Now to the power of God su-preme Be ev-er-last-ing hon-ors given;

3. 'Twas his own pur-pose that be-gan.... To res-cue reb-els doomed to die;

He saves from hell,—we bless his name,— He guides our wand'ring feet.... to heaven.

He gave us grace in Christ, his Son, Be-fore he spread the star-ry sky.

DUET.—BASS & CONTRALTO.

2. Not for our du-ties or de-serts, But of his own a-bound-ing grace,

4. Je-sus, the Lord, ap-pears at last,.... And makes his Father's coun-sels known;

He works sal-va-tion in.... our hearts, And forms a peo-ple for.... his praise.

Declares the great trans-ac-tion past,.... And brings im-mor-tal bless-ings down.

Hymn 3. **HUNTINGTON. L. M.** HERZ.

1. Come, gra-cious Lord, de - scend and dwell, By faith and love, in ev - ery breast;

2. Come, fill our hearts with in - ward strength, Make our en - larg - ed souls pos - sess,

Then shall we know, and taste, and feel The joys that can - not be ex - pressed.

And learn the height, and breadth, and length, Of thine e - ter - nal love and grace.

Hymn 303. **CRAWFORD. L. M.** HAYDN.

1. Now be my heart in-spired to sing The glo - ries of.... my Sav-iour King,— Je - sus the Lord; how

2. O'er all the sons of hu - man race, He shines with a.... su - pe - rior grace: Love from his lips di-

heaven - ly fair His form! how bright his beau-ties are! His form! how bright his beau-ties are!

vine - ly flows, And bless-ings all his state compose, And bless-ings all his state compose.

Hymn 468.   **KIRKLAND.   L. M.**   J. P. H.

1. Haste, traveler, haste! the night comes on.   And many a shin - ing   hour is   gone;

3. Oh, yet a shel - ter you may gain,   A   cov - ert from the   wind and rain;

The   storm is gath - 'ring in   the west,   And thou far off   from home and   rest.

A   hid - ing - place,   a   rest,   a   home.   A   ref - uge from the wrath to   come!

2. The   ris - ing tem - pest sweeps the   sky;   The   rains de - scend, 'the winds are high;

4. Then ling - er not   in   all   the   plain;   Flee   for thy life;   the moun - tain gain;

The   wa - ters swell, and death and   fear   Be - set thy path, nor ref - uge near.

Look   not be - hind; make no   de - lay;   Oh, speed thee, speed thee on   thy   way!

Hymn 264.   **COMSTOCK. L. M.**   Hummel. Arr. D. R. Stanford.

1. The spa-cious firm-a-ment on high, With all the blue e-the-real sky,

2. Soon as the even-ing shades pre-vail, The moon takes up the won-drous tale;

And span-gled heavens, a shin-ing frame, Their great O-rig-i-nal pro-claim: The

And night-ly, to the list-ening earth, Re-peats the sto-ry of her birth; While

unwearied sun, from day to day, Does his Cre-a-tor's power dis-play; And

all the stars that round her burn, And all the plan-ets in their turn, Con-

pub-lish-es to ev-ery land The work, the work of an al-might-y hand.

firm the ti-dings as they roll, And spread, and spread the truth from pole to pole.

Hymn 327. **CROSS. L. M.** Rev. J. B. Dykes.

Slow.

1. He dies! the Friend of sin - ners dies; Lo! Sa - lem's daughters weep a - round;

A sol - emn dark - ness veils the skies; A sud - den trem - bling shakes the ground.

Hymn 327. **HURSLEY. L. M.** Arr. by Monk.

2. Here's love and grief be - yond de - gree: The Lord of glo - ry dies for men;

But, lo! what sud - den joys we see! Je - sus, the dead, re - vives a - gain.

Hymn 445. **BRESLAU. L. M.** Mendelssohn, arr. by Monk.

1. What shall the dy - ing sin - ner do, That seeks re - lief for all his woe?

Where shall the guilt - y conscience find Ease for the tor - ment of the mind?

Hymn 556.   COLOMB.   L. M.   KŒLLA.

1. Wea-ry of wandering from my God, And now made will-ing to re-turn,

2. O Je-sus, full of truth and grace,— More full of grace than I of sin;

I hear, and bow me to the rod: Yet not in hope-less grief I mourn;

Yet once a-gain I seek thy face, O-pen thine arms, and take me in!

I have an ad-vo-cate a-bove, A friend be-fore the throne of love.

And free-ly my back-slid-ings heal, And love thy faith-less serv-ant still.

Hymn 145.   UPSON.   L. M. 6l.   W. H. MONK.

1. Let glo-ry be to God on high: Peace be on earth as in the sky; Good will to men! We bow the knee.

2. We praise, we bless, we worship thee; We give thee thanks, thy name we sing, Almighty Father! Heavenly King!

Hymn 1240.   ETERNITY.   L. M. 7 l.   J. P. H.

1. E - ter - ni - ty! e - ter - ni - ty! How long art thou, e - ter - ni - ty!
2. E - ter - ni - ty! e - ter - ni - ty! How long art thou, e - ter - ni - ty!

p   *f*   *f*

3. E - ter - ni - ty! e - ter - ni - ty! How long art thou, e - ter - ni - ty!

And yet to thee time | hastes a - | way, Like as the war horse | to the | fray,
As long as God is | God, so | long Endure the pains of | hell and | wrong,

O man, full oft thy | tho'ts should | dwell Upon the pains of | sin and | hell,

(Or swift as the couriers homeward go,)
(Or ships to port, or ....)   shaft from | bow; Pon - der, O | man, e - ter - ni - | ty!
(So long the joys of heaven remain;)
(Oh, lasting joy; oh, ...)   last - ing | pain! Pon - der, O | man, e - ter - ni - | ty!

cres. . . . .   *ff*   *p*

(And on the glories of the pure,)
(That do beyond all ....)   time en - | dure; Pon - der, O | man, e - ter - ni - | ty!

Hymn 1118.   HENRY.   C. L. M.   J. P. H.

1. For - get thy - self! Christ bade thee come To think up - on his love,
2. For - get thy - self! and think what pain, What ag - o - ny he bore,

p

3. For - get thy - self! but let thy soul With mem - o - ries o'er - flow,

HENRY. Concluded.

Which could re - verse the sin - ner's doom, And write his name a - bove;
To wash a - way each guilt - y stain, To bless thee ev - er - more:

Re - joice in his su - preme con - trol, And seek his will to know:

Did the re - turn - ing reb - el live, And free - ly all his sins for - give.
To fit thee for his high a - bode, The tem - ple of the liv - ing God,

With thankful heart ap - proach the feast, And thou wilt be a wel - come guest.

Hymn 320. **RUTHVEN. C. L. M.** J. P. H.

1. (He knelt: the Saviour knelt and prayed, When but his) Fa - ther's eye (Looked thro' the lonely garden's shade, On....) that dread ag - o - ny;

2. (The sun set in a fearful hour, The skies might....) well grow dim, (When this mortality had power So......) to o'er - shad - ow him!

The Lord of all a - bove, be - neath, Was bowed with sor - row un - to death.

That he who gave man's breath might know The ver - y depths of hu - man woe.

DURYEA. C. M.

1. Chil-dren of God, who, faint and slow, Your pil-grim-path pur-sue, In strength and weakness,
2. Oh! weak to know a Sav-iour's power, To feel a Father's care; A moment's toil, a

3. And, bursting thro' the dusk-y shroud That dared his power in-vest, Ride throned in light o'er

joy and woe, To God's high call-ing true, To God's, to God's high call-ing
pass-ing shower, Is all the grief ye share, Is all, is all the grief ye

ev-ery cloud, Tri-umph-ant to his rest, Tri-umph-ant to his rest, his

true!— Why move ye thus, with lingering tread, A doubt-ing mournful band? Why
share. The orb of light, though clouds a-while May hide his noon-tide ray, Shall

rest. Then, Christian, dry the fall-ing tear, The faith-less doubt re-move; Re-

faint-ly hangs the droop-ing head? Why fails the fee-ble hand? Why
soon in love-lier beau-ty smile To gild the clos-ing day,— Shall

Sostenuto.

deemed at last from guilt and fear, Oh! wake thy heart to love. Re-

DURYEA. Concluded.

faint - ly hangs the droop - ing head ? Why fails the fee - ble hand ?
soon in love - lier beau - ty smile To gild the clos - ing day,—

deemed at last from guilt and fear, Oh ! wake thy heart to love.

Hymn 553. **CUTHBERT. C. M.** Rev. J. B. Dykes.

1. O thou, from whom all good - ness flows, I lift my soul to thee;

In all my sor - rows, con - flicts, woes, O Lord, re - mem - ber me !

Hymn 417. **ROLLINS. C. M.** Redhead.

1. E - ter - nal Spir - it, God of truth, Our con - trite hearts in - spire;

Re - vive the flame of heaven - ly love, And feed the pure de - sire.

Hymn 833.   **HAZARD. C. M.**   Schubert.

DUET.

1. Our blest Re - deem - er, ere he breathed His ten - der, last fare - well,

3. He came, sweet in - fluence to im - part, A gra - cious, will - ing Guest,

ORGAN.

A Guide, a Com - fort - er bequeathed, With us on earth to dwell.

While he can find one hum - ble heart Where - in to fix his rest.

2. He came in tongues of liv - ing flame, To teach, con - vince, sub - due;

4. And his that gen - tle voice we hear, Soft as the breath of even,

All - power - ful as the wind he came, And all as view - less, too.

That checks each fault, calms ev - ery fear, And whis - pers us of heaven.

Hymn 922.　　　　EATON.　C. M.　　　Arranged.

1. I heard the voice of Je - sus say,— "Come un - to me and rest ;....
D. C. I came to Je - sus as I was, Wea - ry, and worn, and sad,....

2. I heard the voice of Je - sus say,— "Be - hold, I free - ly give....
D. C. I came to Je - sus, and I drank Of that life - giv - ing stream ;

Lay down, thou wea - ry one, lay down Thy head up - on thy breast !"
I found in him a rest - ing - place, And he hath made me glad....

Fine.

The liv - ing wa - ter; thirst - y one, Stoop down, and drink, and live !"..
My thirst was quenched, my soul re - vived, And now I live in him.....

Solo. Soprano.

I came to Je - sus as I was, Wea - ry, and worn, and sad,....
I came to Je - sus, and I drank Of that life - giv - ing stream ;

I found in him a rest - ing - place, And he hath made me glad......
My thirst was quenched, my soul re - vived, And now I live in him......

D. C.

ritard.　　*a tempo.*

PORTER. **C. M.** Concone.

Allegro.

1. Fa - ther of glo - ry! to thy name Im - mor - tal praise we give,....

3. To thine al - might - y Spir - it be Im - mor - tal glo - ry given,....

Who dost an act of grace pro - claim, And bid us reb - els live.....

Whose in - fluence brings us near to thee, And trains us up for heaven...

2. Im - mor - tal hon - or to the Son Who makes thine an - ger cease;...

4. Let men with their u - nit - ed voice A - dore th' e - ter - nal God;....

Our lives he ran - somed with his own, And died to make our peace.....

And spread his hon - ors and their joys Through na - tions far a - broad.....

Hymn 639.　　　**ANDREWS.　C. M.**　　　Rossini.

1. As pants the hart for cool - ing streams, When heat - ed in the chase,

3. Why rest - less, why cast down, my soul? Trust God; who will em - ploy

So longs my soul, O God, for thee, And thy re - fresh - - ing grace.

His aid for thee, and change these sighs To thank - ful hymns... of joy.

Solo. Soprano.

2. For thee, my God— the liv - ing God,.... My thirst-y soul doth pine ;........

4. I sigh to think of hap - pier days, .. When thou, O Lord !.. wast nigh ;........

Oh, when shall I be - hold thy face, Thou Maj - es - ty...... di - vine !

When ev - ery heart was tuned to praise, And none more blest.... than I....

Hymn 271.   **CUYLER.**   **C. M.**   Arranged

Allegro.

1. Fa-ther of glo-ry! to thy name   Im-mor-tal praise we give,....

3. To thine al-might-y Spir-it be   Im-mor-tal glo-ry given,....

Who dost an act of grace pro-claim, And bid us reb-els live,.....

Whose in-fluence brings us near to thee, And trains us up for heaven....

2. Im-mor-tal hon-or to the Son Who makes thine an-ger cease;....

4. Let men with their u-nit-ed voice A-dore th'e-ter-nal God; ....

Our lives he ran-somed with his own, And died to make our peace.....

And spread his hon-ors and their joys Through na-tions far a-broad......

HOWARD. C. M.

1. My Shep-herd will sup-ply my need, Je-ho-vah is his name;

2. When I walk through the shades of death, Thy pres-ence is my stay;...

In pas-tures fresh he makes me feed, Be-side the liv-ing stream.

A word of thy sup-port-ing breath Drives all my fears a-way,....

He brings my wan-dering spir-it back, When I for-sake his ways;

Thy hand, in sight of all my foes, Doth still my ta-ble spread;

And leads me, for his mer-cy's sake, In paths of truth and grace.

My cup with bless-ings o-ver-flows, Thine oil a-noints my head...

Hymn 841. HARRIS. C. M. Arranged.

1. Au-thor of good! to thee we turn: Thine ev-er-wake-ful eye......

2. Oh, let thy love with-in us dwell, Thy fear our foot-steps guide;....

A-lone can all.... our wants dis-cern— Thy hand a-lone sup-ply......

That love shall vain - er loves ex-pel, That fear, all fears be-side......

Hymn 190. CLINTON. C. M. J. P. H.

1. Blest are the souls that hear and know The gos-pel's joy-ful sound;

2. Their joy shall bear their spir-its up Through their Re-deem-er's name;

Peace shall at-tend the path they go, And light their steps sur-round.

His right-eous-ness ex-alts their hope, Nor Sa-tan dares con-demn.

TRUMAN. C. M. J. P. H.

1. Thou art my hid-ing-place, O Lord! In thee I put my trust;

2. When storms of fierce temp-ta-tion beat, And fu-rious foes as-sail,

En - couraged by thy ho - ly word, A fee - ble child of dust:

My ref - uge is the mer - cy - seat, My hope with-in the vail:

I have no ar - gu - ment be - side, I urge no oth - er plea;

From strife of tongues, and bit - ter words, My spir - it flies to thee;

And 't is e - nough my Sav - iour died, My Sav - iour died for me!

Joy to my heart the thought af - fords, My Sav - iour died for me!

Hymn 790.   **ADAMS.   C. M.**   Arranged.

1. Thou art.... my ·hid-ing-place, O Lord! In thee.... I put my trust;....

2. When storms of fierce tempt-a-tion beat, And fu-rious foes as-sail,.....

En-cour-aged by thy ho-ly word, A.... fee-ble child of dust:

My ref-uge is the mer-cy-seat, My.... hope with-in the vail;

1. I have no ar-gu-ment be-side, I urge no oth-er plea;

f   *tenuto.*

2. From strife of tongues, and bit-ter words, My spir-it flies to thee;

And 'tis.... e-nough my Sav-iour died, My Sav-iour died for me!

                                        rall.

Joy to..... my heart the thought af-fords, My Sav-iour died for me!

Hymn 87. **FINCKE. C. M.** SPOHR.

Andante.

Ona. *p* ... *cres.*

1. A - gain the Lord of life and light A - wakes the kind - ling ray,......... Dis - pels the

2. Oh, what a night was that which wrapt A guilt - y world in gloom!...... Oh, what a

dark - ness of the night, Dis - pels the dark - ness of the night, And pours in - creas - ing day.

sun which broke this day, Oh, what a sun which broke this day Tri - umph - ant from the tomb!

Hymn 466. **ROBERTS. C. M.** REDHEAD.

1. Lord, we a - dore thy bound - less grace, The heights and depths un - known,

Of par - don, life, and joy, and peace, In thy be - lov - ed Son.

Hymn 558. **STRINGHAM. C. M.** Arranged.

1. Oh, for a heart to praise my God, A heart from sin set free;

3. Oh, for a low - ly, con - trite heart, Be - liev - ing, true, and clean!

A heart that's sprink - led with the blood So free - ly shed for me!

Which nei - ther life nor death can part From him that dwells with - in.

2. A heart re - signed, sub - miss - ive, meek, My dear Re - deem - er's throne;

4. A heart in ev - ery thought re - newed, And filled with love di - vine;

5. Thy na - ture, gra - cious Lord! im - part; Come quick - ly from a - bove; *

* See next page for close of verse 5.

Where on - ly Christ is heard to speak, Where Je - sus reigns a - lone!

Per - fect, and right, and pure, and good; An im - age, Lord! of thine.

STRINGHAM. Concluded.

Ending for verse 5

Write thy new name up-on my heart,— Thy new, best name of love.

Write thy new name up-on my heart,— Thy new, best name of love.

Hymn 790. **PACKER.** C. M. J. P. H.

1. Thou art my hid-ing-place, O Lord! In thee I put my trust; En-cour-aged by thy

pp tempo.

2. When storms of fierce tempt-a-tion beat, And fu-rious foes as-sail, My ref-uge is the

ho-ly word, A fee-ble child of dust: I have no ar-gu-ment be-side, I

rit. f *pp tempo.* *f*

mer-cy-seat, My hope with-in the vail: From strife of tongues, and bit-ter words, My

urge no oth-er plea; And 'tis e-nough my Sav-iour died, My Sav-iour died for me!

spir-it flies to thee; Joy to my heart the thought af-fords, My Sav-iour died for me!

Hymn 553.   **THORNE.**   **C. M.**   L. De Call.

1. O thou, from whom all good - ness flows, I lift my soul to thee;

1. O thou, from whom all good - ness flows, I lift my soul to thee:

In all my sor - rows, con - flicts, woes, O Lord, re - mem - ber me!

In all my sor - rows, con - flicts, woes, O Lord, re - mem - ber me!

2. When on my ach - ing, bur - dened heart My sins lie heav - i - ly,

2. When on my ach - ing, bur - dened heart My sins lie heav - i - ly,

Thy par - don grant, new peace im - part; Thus, Lord, re - mem - ber me!

Thy par - don grant, new peace im - part; Thus, Lord, re - mem - ber me!

THORNE. Concluded.

3. When tri - als sore ob - struct my way, And ills I can - not flee, Oh, let my strength be

3. When tri - als sore ob - struct my way, And ills I can - not flee, Oh, let my strength be

as my day— Dear Lord, re - mem - ber me! 4. When in the sol - emn

as my day— Dear Lord, re - mem - ber me! 4. When in the sol - emn

hour of death I wait thy just de - cree; Be this the prayer of my last breath:

hour of death I wait thy just de - cree; Be this the prayer of my last breath:

Now, Lord, re - mem - ber me! Now, Lord, now Lord, re - mem - ber me!

Now, Lord, re - mem - ber me! Now, Lord, now Lord, re - mem - ber me!

Hymn 269. **GRIFFITH. C. M.** J. P. H.

DUET.—TENOR & CONTRALTO.

1. Lord, when my rap - tured thought sur - veys Cre - a - tion's beau - ties o'er....

3. On me thy prov - i - dence has shone With gen - tle smil - ing rays;....

All na - ture joins to teach thy praise, And bid my soul a - dore.
cres.

Oh, let my lips and life make known Thy good- ness and thy praise

2. Where - e'er I turn my gaz - ing eyes, Thy ra - diant foot - steps shine ;....

4. All - bounteous Lord, thy grace im - part ! Oh, teach me to im - prove....

Ten thousand pleasing wonders rise, And speak their source divine, And speak their source di - vine.
And speak............

Thy gifts with humble, grateful heart, And crown them with thy love, And crown them with thy love.
And crown............

Hymn 725.   **MARIAN.   C. M.**   J. P. H.

1. To thee, my Shep-herd, and my Lord, A grate-ful song I'll raise:

Oh, let the hum-blest of thy flock At-tempt to speak thy praise.

Hymn 943.   **REMSEN.   C. M.**   J. P. H.

1. Fa-ther of mer-cies! send thy grace, All power-ful from a-bove,....

To form, in our o-be-dient souls, The im-age of thy love.....

Hymn 704.   **CHURCH.   C. M.**   J. P. H.

1. Dear Ref-uge of my wea-ry soul, On thee, when sor-rows rise,

On thee, when waves of troub-le roll, My faint-ing hope re-lies.

Hymn 250.   **IVISON.** **C. M. 61.**   Arranged.

1. Be - yond, be - yond the bound - less sea, A - bove that dome of sky,......

2. Art nigh, and yet my la - boring mind Feels af - ter thee in vain—

Fur - ther than thought it - self can flee, Thy dwell - ing is on high:....

Thee in these works of power to find, Or to thy seat at - tain.....

Yet dear the aw - ful thought to me, That thou, my God! art nigh:....

Thy mes - sen - ger— the storm - y wind; Thy path— the track - less main.....

Hymn 376.   **SHERBORNE.** **7s. 61.**   W. H. MONK.

1. Glo - ry, glo - ry to our King! Crowns un - fad - ing wreathe his head;
2. Je - sus is gone up on high, An - gels come to meet their King;

3. Now be - hold him high en - throned, Glo - ry beam - ing from his face!

SHERBORNE. Concluded.

Je - sus is the name we sing— Je - sus, ris - en from the dead ;
Shouts tri! - umph - ant rend the sky, While the vic - tor's praise they sing :

By a - dor - ing an - gels owned. God of ho - li - ness and grace !

Je - sus, con - qu'ror o'er the grave ; Je - sus, might - y now to save,
"O - pen now, ye heaven - ly gates ! 'Tis the King of glo - ry waits."

Oh, for hearts and tongues to sing "Glo - ry, glo - ry to our King !"

Hymn 423. **STUART. C. M.** DRETSHOCK.

1. Spir - it of peace, ce - les - tial Dove, How ex - cel - lent thy praise !....
2. Sweet as the dew on hill and flower, That si - lent - ly dis - tills,......

How rich the gift of Chris - tian love Thy gra - cious power dis - plays !...
At even - ing's soft and balm - y hour, On Zi - on's fruit - ful hills.....

Hymn 841. *KITTREDGE. C. M.

Abt, arr. by D. R. Stanford.

1. Au - thor of good! to thee we turn: Thine ev - er wake - ful eye
Duet. p

3. And since by pas - sion's force sub - dued, Too oft, with stub - born will,

A - lone can all our wants dis - cern — Thy hand a - lone sup - ply.
p   f

We blind - ly shun the la - tent good, And grasp the spe - cious ill;—

2. Oh, let thy love with - in us dwell, Thy fear our foot - steps guide;......
f   pp   f   pp

4. Not what we wish, but what we want, Let mer - cy still sup - ply......

That love shall vain - er loves ex - pel, That fear, that fear, all fears be - side.
p   pp

The good we ask not, Fa - ther, grant: The ill we ask de - ny, de - ny.

* Or Hymn 375. C. L. M. by repeating the last two lines.

Hymn 566. **LOOMIS. C. M.** J. P. H.

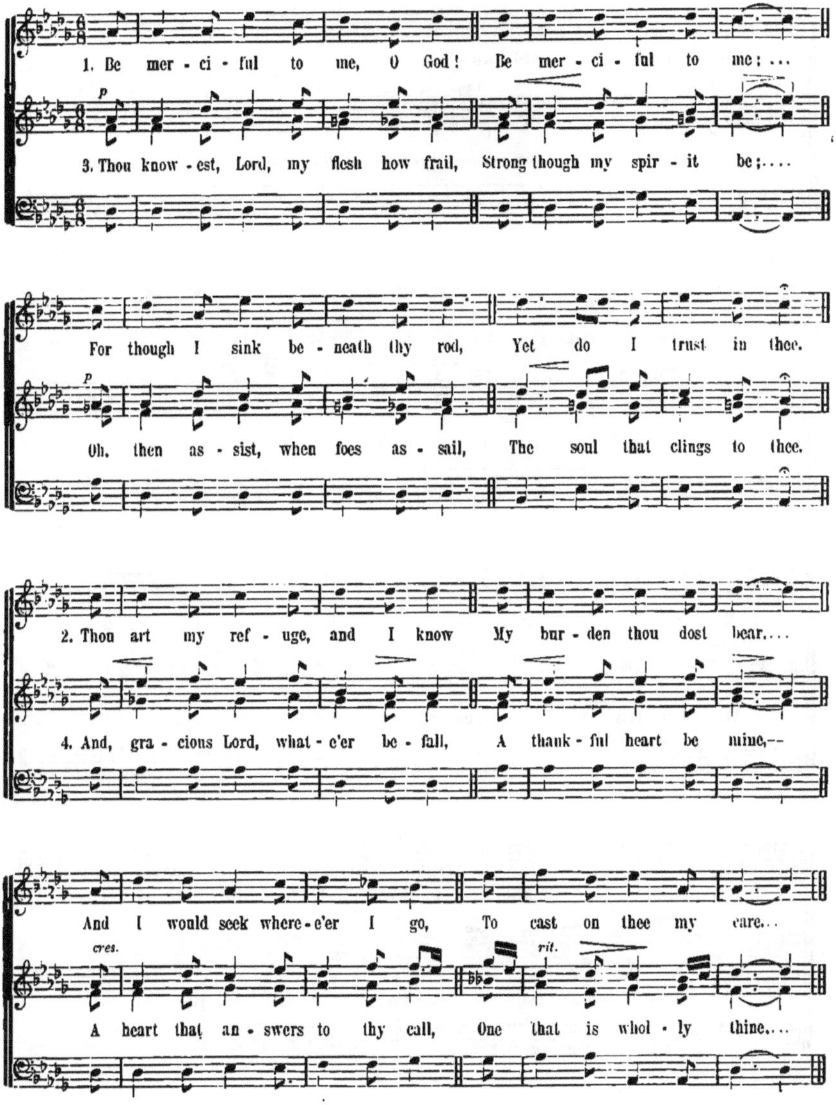

Hymn 226.   **BISCHOFF. C. M.**   J. P. H.

1. When morn - ing's first and hal - lowed ray Breaks, with its trem - bling light,...

3. When even - ing's si - lent shades de - scend, And na - ture sinks to rest,...

To chase the pearl - y dews a - way, Bright tear - drops of the night.—

Still, to my Fa - ther and my Friend, My wish - es are ad - dressed.

Duet. Tenor and Soprano.

2. My heart, O Lord! for - gets to rove, But ris - es glad - ly free,....

Soprano.

4. Tho' tears may dim my hours of joy, And bid my pleas - ures flee,....

On wings of ev - er - last - ing love, And finds its home in thee,....

Thou reign'st where grief can - not an - noy; I will be glad in thee,....

Hymn 466. SOUTHWELL. C. M. H. S. IRONS.

1. Lord, we a - dore thy bound-less grace, The heights and depths un - known,

Of par - don, life, and joy, and peace, In thy be - lov - ed Son.

Hymn 465. STOCKTON. C. M. T. WRIGHT.

1. The Sav - iour calls! let ev - ery ear At - tend the heaven - ly sound:

Ye doubt - ing souls, dis - miss your fear; Hope smiles re - viv - ing round.

Hymn 233. HEATH. C. M. J. P. H.

1. Great God! how in - fi - nite art thou! What worth - less worms are we!

Let the whole race of creat - ures bow, And pay their praise to thee.

Hymn 1177. BEECHER. C. M. J. P. H.

1. It came up-on   the mid - night clear,   That glo - rious song of   old,

2. Still through the clo - ven skies   they   come,   With peace-ful wings un - furled ;

From an - gels bend - ing   near   the   earth   To   touch their harps   of   gold ;

And   still ce - les - tial mu - sic   floats   O'er   all   the wea - ry   world ;

"Peace   to   the earth,   good - will   to   man,   From heaven's all-gracious   King :"

A - bove   its   sad   and   low - ly   plains   They bend on heavenly   wing,

The   earth in sol - emn still - ness   lay,   To   hear the an - gels   sing,

And ev - er o'er   its Ba - bel   sounds,   The bless - ed an - gels   sing.

BEECHER. Concluded.

The earth in sol - emn still - ness lay, To hear the an - gels sing.

And ev - er o'er its Ba - bel sounds, The bless - ed an - gels sing,

3 O ye, beneath life's crushing load,
   Whose forms are bending low,
Who toil along the climbing way,
   With painful steps and slow ;—
Look up ! for glad and golden hours
   Come swiftly on the wing ;
Oh, rest beside the weary road,
   And hear the angels sing !

4 For lo ! the days are hastening on,
   By prophet-bards foretold,
When with the ever-circling years
   Comes round the age of gold !
When peace shall over all the earth
   Its final splendors fling,
And the whole world send back the song
   Which now the angels sing !

Hymn 787.   **HURLBUT. 8,8,8,6.**   Flemming.
Arr. by D. R. Stanford.

Legato.

1. O Ho - ly Sav - iour! Friend un - seen, Since on thine arm thou bid'st me lean,

2. Blest with this fel - low - ship di - vine, Take what thou wilt, I'll not re - pine;

pp

Help me, throughout life's chang - ing scene, By faith to cling to thee !

For, as the branch - es to the vine, My soul would cling to thee.

f   pp

Hymn 384.   **ROBINSON. C. M.**   J. P. H.

DUET.—BASS & CONTRALTO.

1. The gold - en gates are lift - ed up, The doors are o - pened wide,

4. Lift up our hearts, lift up our minds, Let thy dear grace be given,

ORG.

The King of glo - ry is gone in Un - to his Fa - ther's side.

That while we tar - ry here be - low, Our treas - ure be in heaven!

ORG.

DUET.   QUARTET.

2. Thou art gone up be - fore us, Lord, To make for us a place,

5. That where thou art, at God's right hand, Our hope, our love may be;

Fine.

That we may be where now thou art, And look up - on God's face.

Fine. ad lib.

Dwell thou in us, that we may dwell For - ev - er - more in thee!

ROBINSON. Concluded. BELLINI. **69**

3. And ev-er on.... thine earth-ly path A gleam of glo - ry lies;.........

A light still breaks be - hind the cloud That vailed, that vailed thee from our eyes.

Hymn 641.   **KELLOGG. C. M.**   Schubert.

1. Oh! could our thoughts and wish - es fly,   A - bove these gloom - y shades,

3. Lord! send   a   beam   of   light   di - vine,   To guide   our   up - ward   aim;

To   those   bright worlds, be - yond   the   sky,   Which sor - row ne'er   in - vades!—

With one   re - viv - ing touch   of   thine,   Our   lan - guid hearts   in - flame.

2. There, joys,   un - seen   by mor - tal   eyes,   Or   rea - son's fee - ble   ray,

4. Oh! then,   on   faith's sub - lim - est   wing,   Our   ar - dent hope shall   rise

In   ev - er - bloom - ing   pros - pects riso,   Un - con - scious   of   de - cay.

To   those bright scenes, where pleas - ures spring   Im - mor - tal   in   the   skies.

ONE SWEETLY SOLEMN THOUGHT. J. P. H.

Hymn 1227.

1. One sweetly solemn thought, Comes to me .... | o'er and | o'er—
2. Nearer the bound of life, Where we lay our .... | bur - dens | down :

3. Father, perfect my trust ! Strengthen the .... | might of my | faith ;

I am nearer home to-day Than I ever have .... | been be - | fore.
Nearer leaving the cross ; Nearer .... | gaining the | crown.

Let me feel as I would when I stand On the rock of the .... | shore of | death.

Nearer my Father's house, Where the .... | many mansions | be ;
But lying darkly between, Winding .... | down through the | night,

Feel as I would when my feet, Are .... | slipping over the | brink ;—

Nearer the .... | great white | throne ; Nearer the .... | crys - tal | sea ;—
Is the deep and .... | un - known | stream, That leads at .... | last to the | light.

For it may be, I'm .... | near - er | home— Nearer .... | now than I | think !

Hymn 294.   **LEGGAT. C. M.**   Donizetti.

TENOR SOLO.

A pil - grim through this lone - ly world, The.... bless - ed Sav - iour passed;

A mourner all his life was he, A dy - ing Lamb at last,........

That tender heart that felt for all, For all its life - blood gave:

ritard e piano.

It found on earth no rest - - ing - place, Save on - ly in the grave. ...

Such was our Lord! and shall we fear The cross with all its scorn? Or love a faith-less

Such was our Lord! and shall we fear The cross with all its scorn? Or love a faith-less

e - vil world, That wreathed his brow with thorn? No! fa - cing all its frowns or smiles, Like him o -

e - vil world, That wreathed his brow with thorn? No! fa - cing all its frowns or smiles, Like him o -

be - dient still, We homeward press thro' storm or calm, To Zi - on's bless - ed hill.

be - dient still, We homeward press thro' storm or calm, To Zi - on's bless - ed hill.

Hymn 961.   TROYTE.   8,8,8,4.   A. H D. Troyte.

1. My God, my Father,.... | while I | stray | Far from my home on...... | life's rough | way,

2. What though in lonely.... | grief I | sigh | For friends beloved no...... | long - er | nigh;

Oh, teach me from my | heart to | say, | "Thy | will be | done!" | A - | men.

Submissive still would | I re - | ply, | "Thy | will be | done!" | A - | men.

CLOSE.

Hymn 785.   ABIDE WITH ME.   10s.   J. P. H.

1. A - | bide with | me! | Fast falls the eventide, The darkness deepens—Lord, with | me a - | bide!
2. A - | bide with | me! | Swift to its close ebbs out life's little day; Earth's joys grow dim, its glories.. | pass a - | way;

3. A - | bide with | me! | I need thy presence every passing hour; What but thy grace can foil the...... | tempter's | power?
4. A - | bide with | me! | Not a brief glance I long, a passing word, But as thou dwell'st with thy dis - - - - - - - | ci - ples, | Lord.

When other helpers fail, and | comforts | flee, | Help of the helpless, oh, a - | bide with | me!
Change and decay in all a - | round I | see; | O thou, who changest not, a - | bide with | me!

Who, like thyself my guide and | stay can | be? | Through cloud and sunshine, oh, a - | bide with | me!
Familiar, condescending,........ | pa - tient, | free, | Come, not to sojourn, but a - | bide with | me!

Hymn 462.   **TIPSTANLEY.**   **S. M.**   Arr. Rossini.

1. Come to the land of peace;.... From shad - ows come a - way;....

2. Fear hath no dwell - ing here;.... But pure re - pose and love....

Where all the sounds of weep - ing cease, And storms no more have sway.

Breathe thro' the bright, ce - les - tial air The spir - it of the dove.

Hymn 148.   **HAYDN.**   **S. M.**   Haydn.

1. The Lord Je - ho - vah reigns, Let all the na - tions fear;

2. In Zi - on stands his throne, His hon - ors are di - vine;

Let sin - ners trem - ble at his throne, And saints be hum - ble there.

His Church shall make his won - ders known, For there his glo - ries shine.

Hymn 835.   **GLEASON. S. M.**   J. P. H.

1. Oh, bless the Lord, my soul! Let all with-in me join,

3. 'Tis he for-gives thy sins; 'Tis he re-lieves thy pain;

And aid my tongue to bless his name, Whose fa - vors are di - vine.

'Tis he that heals thy sick - ness-es, And makes thee young a-gain.

2. Oh, bless the Lord, my soul!... Nor let his mer - cies lie

4. He crowns thy life with love,... When ran - somed from the grave;

For - got - ten in un - thank - ful - ness, And with-out prais - es die.

He, who re - deemed my soul from hell, Hath sov - ereign power to save.

FOSTER. S. M. FRANZ.

1. Thou Lord of all a - bove, And all be - low the sky, Pros - trate be - fore thy

mf

4. The bur - den which I feel, Thou on - ly canst re - move; Dis - play, O Lord! thy

feet I fall, And for thy mer - cy cry. 2. For - give my fol - lies

p *mf*

par - doning grace, And thy un - bound - ed love. Org. 5. One gra - cious look of

past, The crimes which I have done; Oh! bid a con - trite sin - ner live,

mf *p*

thine Will ease my troub - led breast; Oh! let me know my sins for - given,

Oh! bid a con - trite sin - ner live, Thro' thy, thro' thy in - carn - ate Son.

pp *f* *p*

Oh! let me know my sins for - given, And I, and I shall then be blest.

Hymn 261. **NEWBERRY. S. M.** Rossini.

1. Oh, bless the Lord, my soul! His grace to thee pro - claim; And all that is with-

3. He will not al - ways chide; He will with pa - tience wait; His wrath is ev - er

in me join To bless his ho - ly name. 2. Oh! bless the Lord, my soul!....

slow to rise, And read - y to a - bate. 4. He par - dons all thy sins,....

His mer - cies bear in mind; For - get not all his ben - e - fits: The

Pro - longs thy fee - ble breath; He heal - eth thy in - firm - i - ties. And

Lord to thee is kind, The Lord to thee is kind, The Lord to thee is kind.

ran-soms thee from death, And ran-soms thee from death, And ran-soms thee from death.

Hymn 85.   TURNER.   S. M.   J. P. II.

CONTRALTO SOLO.

1. Come   to the house of prayer,   O thou af - flict - ed,;   come;
3. Ye · a - ged, hith - er come,   For ye have felt his   love;

ORG.

The God   of   peace shall meet thee there— He makes that house.. his home.
Soon shall your tremb-ling tongues be dumb, Your lips for - get.. to move.

SW. ORGAN.   cres.   rit. colla voce.   p

2. Come   to the house of praise.   Ye who are hap - py now;

mf

4. Ye young, be - fore   his throne.   Come, bow; your voi - ces raise;

In sweet ac - cord your voi - ces raise,   In kin - dred hom - age bow.

pp

Let not your hearts his praise dis - own   Who gives the power to praise.

Hymn 1023.   **IDE.   S. M.**   German.

Quartet.

1. Far as thy name is known. The world de - clares thy praise;

2. Let stran - gers walk a - round The cit - y where we dwell,

Thy saints, O Lord, be - fore thy throne, Their songs of.... hon - or raise.

Duet.

Com - pass and view thine ho - ly ground, And mark the... build - ing well—

Chorus.

With joy thy peo - ple stand On Zi - on's chos - en hill,

The or - der of thy house, The wor - ship of thy court,

Pro - claim the won - ders of thy hand, And coun - sels of thy will.

The cheer - ful songs, the sol - emn vows; And make a fair re - port.

Hymn 261. **VINING. S. M.** J. P. H.

Andante.

1. Oh, bless the Lord, my soul! His grace to thee pro - claim;

mf

3. He will not al - ways chide; He will with pa - tience wait:

And all that is with - in me join To bless his ho - ly name.

cres.

His wrath is ev - er slow to rise, And read - y to a - bate.

2. Oh, bless the Lord, my soul!.... His mer - cies bear in mind:

p   *p*

4. He par - dons all thy sins,..... Pro - longs thy fee - ble breath;

For - get not all his ben - e - fits: The Lord to thee is kind.

cres.   *f*

He heal - eth thy in - firm - i - ties, And ran - soms thee from death.

Hymn 636.   **ALLEN. S. M.**   MERCADANTE.

1. I want a heart to pray— To pray and nev-er cease;
2. I want a true re-gard, A sin-gle, stead-y aim—

Nev-er to mur-mur at thy stay,.... Or wish my suf-ferings less,
Un-moved by threatening or re-ward,... To thee and thy great name;

rit.

1. This bless-ing, a-bove all-- Al-ways to pray— I want;

ff

2. A jeal-ous, just con-cern, For thine im-mor-tal praise;

Out of the deep on thee to call, And nev-er, nev-er faint.

p   *rit.*

A pure de-sire that all may learn And glo-ri-fy thy grace.

Hymn 163. **NORTHRUP. S. M.** S. H. MERLIS.

1. Our Heaven - ly Fa - ther, hear The prayer we of - fer now:

2. Thy king - dom come; thy will On earth be done in love,

Thy name be hal - lowed far and near, To thee all na - tions bow.

As saints and ser - a - phim ful - fill Thy per - fect law a - bove.

Hymn 446. **MINER. S. M.** J. P. H.

1. Like sheep.... we went a - stray, And broke the fold of God;.....

2. How dread - ful was the hour, When God our wan - derings laid,......

Each wan - dering in a dif - ferent way, But all the down - ward road.

And did.... at once his venge - ance pour Up - on the Shep - herd's head!

Hymn 847. **LEONARD. S. M.** Spohr.

1. Blest be the tie that binds Our hearts in Chris - tian love;

2. Be - fore our Fa - ther's throne We pour our ar - dent prayers;

The fel - low - ship of kin - dred minds Is like to that a - bove.

Our fears, our hopes, our aims are one, Our com - forts and our cares.

Hymn 1239. **EDWARDS. S. M.** Beethoven.

Unison.

1. And will the Judge de - scend, And must the dead a - rise,

2. How will my heart en - dure The ter - rors of that day,

Org.

And not a sin - gle soul es - cape His all - dis - cern - ing eyes?

When earth and heaven be - fore his face As - ton - ished shrink a - way?

Hymn 489. **WANDERER. S. M.** J. P. H.

1. Oh! where shall rest be found— Rest for the wea - ry soul?

2. The world can nev - er give....... The bliss for which we sigh:

'Twere vain the o - cean depths to sound, Or pierce to ei - ther pole.

'Tis not the whole of life to live, Nor all of death to die.

Hymn 729. **KEITH. S. M.** GANZBACH.

1. My spir - it on thy care...... Blest Sav - iour, I re - cline,

2. What - e'er e - vents be - tide,...... Thy will they all per - form;..

Thou wilt not leave me to de - spair, For thou art love di - vine.

Safe in thy breast my head I hide, Nor fear the com - ing storm.

Hymn 1273. STRICKLAND. S. M. J. P. H.

1. There is no night in heaven; In that blest world a - bove Work nev - er can bring

2. There is no want in heaven; The Lamb of God sup - plies Life's tree of twelve-fold

wea - ri - ness, For work it - self is love. There is no grief in heaven; For life is

fruit - age still, Life's spring which nev - er dries. There is no sin in heaven; Be - hold that

one glad day, And tears are of those for - mer things Which all have passed a - way.

bless - ed throng! All ho - ly is their spot - less robe, All ho - ly is their song.

Hymn 1028. SEVERANCE. S. M. Hesse.

1. How beau-teous are their feet Who stand on Zi - on's hill! .... Who bring sal - va - tion

3. How hap - py are our ears, That hear this joy - ful sound! .. Which kings and proph-ets

SEVERANCE. Concluded.

on their tongues, And words of peace re-veal. 2. How charming is their voice! How

wait-ed for, And sought, but nev-er found. 4. How bless-ed are our eyes, That

sweet their ti-dings are! "Zi-on, be-hold thy Sav-iour King; He reigns and tri-umphs here."

see this heavenly light! Proph-ets and kings de-sired it long, But died with-out the sight.

Hymn 462. **TODD. S. M.** J. P. H.

1. Come to the land of peace; From shad-ows come a-way;

2. Fear hath no dwell-ing here; But pure re-pose and love

Where all the sounds of weep-ing cease, And storms no more have sway,

Breathe through the bright, ce-les-tial air The spir-it of the dove.

Hymn 291. **FIELD. H. M.** J. P. H.

1. Hark! hark!—the notes of joy Roll o'er the heaven-ly plains, And ser - aphs find em-

2. Hark! hark!—the sounds draw nigh, The joy - ful hosts de - scend; Je - sus for - sakes the

ploy... For their sub - lim - est strains; Some new de - light in heaven is known:

sky,... To earth his foot-steps bend: He comes to bless our fall - en race;

Loud sound the harps... a - round the throne; Some new de - light in

He comes with mes - sa - ges of grace: He comes to bless our

heaven.. is known; Loud sound the harps.... a - round the throne.

fall - - en race; He comes with mes - - sa - ges of grace.

Hymn 268. **LYMAN. H. M.** BEETHOVEN.

1. The prom-is-es I sing, Which sov-'reign love hath spoke; Nor will th'e-ter-nal King

2. The mount-ains melt a-way When once the Judge ap-pears, And sun and moon de-cay,

His words of grace re-voke: They stand se-cure And stead-fast

They stand se - - cure And stead - fast

That meas-ure mor-tal years; But still the same, In ra-diant

still; Not Zi-on's hill A- -bides so sure.

still; Not Zi- -on's hill

lines The prom-ise shines Through all the flame.

Hymn 1235. **ST. PHILIP. 7s. 3l.** MONK.

1. Day of an-ger! that dread day Shall the sign in heaven dis-play, And the earth in ash-es lay!

2. Oh, what trembling shall ap-pear, When his com-ing shall be near, Who shall all things strictly clear!

Hymn 416. **ATWATER. H. M.** J. P. H.

1. O thou that hear - est prayer! At - tend our hum - ble cry; And
2. If earth - ly par - ents hear Their chil - dren when they cry; If

3. Our heaven - ly Fa - ther thou,— We— chil - dren of thy grace,— Oh,

let thy serv - ants share Thy bless - ing from on high: We plead the
they, with love sin - cere, Their chil - dren's wants sup - ply; Much more will

let thy Spir - it now De - scend and fill the place; That all may

prom - ise of...... thy word, Grant us thy Ho - ly Spir - it, Lord!
thou thy love... dis - play, And an - swer when thy chil - dren pray.

feel the heaven - ly flame And all u - nite to praise thy name.

Hymn 268. **VAUGHAN. H. M.** Donizetti.

1. The prom - is - es I sing, Which sovereign love hath spoke; Nor will th'e - ter - nal

2. The mountains melt a - way When once the Judge ap - pears, And sun and moon de-

VAUGHAN. Concluded.

King .... His words of grace re - voke: They stand se - cure And steadfast still;

cay, ... That measure mor - tal years; But still the same In ra - diant lines

Not Zi - on's hill A - bides so sure, Not Zi - on's hill A - bides so sure.

The promise shines Thro' all the flame, The prom - ise shines Thro' all the flame.

Hymn 139. FISKE. S. P. M. J. P. H.

1. The Lord Je - ho - vah reigns, And roy - al state maintains, His head with aw - ful glories crowned:
2. Up - held by thy commands, The world se - cure - ly stands, And skies and stars o - bey thy word;

3. Thy prom - is - es are true, Thy grace is ev - er new; There fixed, thy church shall ne'er re - move;

Ar - rayed in robes of light, Be - girt with sovereign might, And rays of maj - es - ty a - round.
Thy throne was fixed on high Ere stars adorned the sky: E - ter - nal is thy kingdom, Lord.

Thy saints with ho - ly fear Shall in thy courts ap - pear, And sing thine ev - er - last - ing love.

Hymn 689. **INGRAHAM. H. M.** Schultz.

Moderato.

1. Fight the good fight! lay hold Up - on e - ter - nal life; Keep but thy shield--be

mf

2. No force of earth or hell, Though fiends with men u - nite, Truth's champion can com -

bold! Stand thro' the hot - test strife; With thy great Captain on the field, Thou canst not fail un -

pel, How - ev - er pressed, to flight: He stands unmoved up - on the field: He can - not fall, un -

less thou yield, With thy great Cap - tain on the field, Thou canst not fail, un - less thou yield.

ff

less he yield, He stands unmoved up - on the field; He can - not fall, un - less he yield.

Hymn 257. **CANFIELD. C. P. M.** J. P. H.

1. My God, thy bound - less love I praise; How bright on high its glo - ries blaze!

mf *f cres.*

2. 'Tis love that paints the pur - ple morn, And bids the clouds in air up - borne,

CANFIELD. Concluded.

DUET.—TENOR & SOPRANO.

How sweet-ly bloom be-low! It streams from thy e-ter-nal throne; Through

pp

Their ge-nial drops dis-til! In ev-ery ver-nal beam it glows, It

f

heaven its joys for-ev-er run. And o'er the earth they flow, And o'er the earth they flow.

cres.

breathes in ev-ery gale that blows, And glides in ev-ery rill. And glides in ev-ery rill.

Hymn 1301. **BEYOND THE SMILING.** J. P. H.

1. Beyond the smiling and the weeping | I shall be | soon; |{Beyond the waking and the sleeping, / Beyond the sowing and the reaping,} | I shall be | soon!

2. Beyond the blooming and the fading, | I shall be | soon; |{Beyond the shining and the shading, / Beyond the hoping and the dreading,} | I shall be | soon!

Love, rest, and home—Sweet hope! Sweet hope! Lord, tar-ry not, but come!

Love, rest, and home—Sweet hope! Sweet hope! Lord, tar-ry not, but come!

Hymn 1290.   **PATTERSON.** 8s & 7s. Peculiar.   J. P. H.

1. Lo, the seal of death is break-ing; Those who slept its sleep are wak-ing;

2. There, no more at eve de-clin-ing, Suns with-out a cloud are shin-ing

Heav-en opes its port-als fair! Heav-en opes its port-als fair!

O'er the land of life and love; O'er the land of life and love:

Hark! the harps of God are ring-ing, Hark! the ser-aph's hymn is fling-ing

There the founts of life are flow-ing, Flowers un-known to time are blow-ing,

Mu - sic on im-mor-tal air, Mu - sic on im-mor-tal air.

In that ra - diant scene a - bove, In that ra - diant scene a - bove.

Hymn 998. EMBURY. `6s. A. Emil Titl.

1. There is a bless-ed home Be - yond this land of woe,

2. There is a land of peace; Good an-gels know it well;

Where tri - als nev - er come, Nor tears of sor - row flow;

Glad songs that nev - er cease With - in its port - als swell;

SOPRANO SOLO. *ritard.*

Where faith is lost 'in sight,.... And pa - tient hope is crowned,

A - round its glo - rious throne ... 'Ten thou - sand saints a - dore

colla voce. *a tempo.*

And ev - er - last - ing light Its glo - ry throws a - - round.

Christ, with the Fa - ther one, And Spir - it, ev - er - - more.

Hymn 998.   BICKNELL.   6s.   FESCA.

1. There is a bless-ed home Be-yond this land of woe, Where tri-als

2. There is a land of peace: Good an-gels know it well; Glad songs that

nev-er come, Nor tears of sor-row flow; Where faith is lost in sight,

nev-er cease With-in its port-als swell; A-round its glo-rious throne

And pa-tient hope is crowned, And ev-er-last-ing light Its glo-ry....

Ten thou-sand saints a-dore Christ, with the Fa-ther one, And Spir-it,....

throws a-round; And ev-er-last-ing light Its glo-ry throws a-round.

ev-er-more: Christ, with the Fa-ther one, And Spir-it ev-er-more.

Hymn 994. **MANSFIELD. 6s.** Taubert.

1. My spir-it longs for thee To dwell with-in my breast;
2. Un-til it come to thee, In vain I look a-round;

Al-though un-wor-thy I Of so di-vine a Guest!
In all that I can see No rest is to be found!

Of so di-vine a Guest Un-wor-thy though I be,
No rest is to be found, But in thy bleed-ing love,

Yet hath my heart no rest Un-til it come to thee!
Oh, let my wish be crowned, And send it from a-bove!

Hymn 992.   **JEWETT.**   **6s.**   WEBER.

1. My Je - sus, as thou wilt! Oh! may thy will be mine; In - to thy hand of love

2. My Je - sus, as thou wilt! Though seen through many a tear, Let not my star of hope

I would my all re - sign; Through sor - row, or through joy, Con - duct me

Grow dim or dis - ap - pear: Since thou on earth hast wept, And sor - rowed

as thine own, And help me still to say My Lord, thy will be done!

oft a - lone, If I must weep with thee, My Lord, thy will be done!

Hymn 926.   **BELCHER.**   **6s & 4s.**   OTTO.

1. Peace, peace, I leave with you, My peace I give to you, My peace I give to you,

2. Peace, peace, I leave with you, My peace I give to you, My peace I give to you,

BELCHER. Concluded.

Trust to my care! Thus the Re-deem-er said, And bowed his sa-cred head,

Per-fect and pure; Not as the world doth give, Words that the soul de-ceive;

Lone in the gar-den shade, Wres-tling in prayer,.... Wres-tling in prayer.

Ye who in me be-lieve Shall rest se-cure,...... Shall rest se-cure.

Hymn 775.　　ELY.　6s & 4s.　　J. P. H.

1. Near-er, my God, to thee, Near-er to thee! Ev'n though it be a cross That rais-eth

2. Though like the wan-der-er, The sun gone down, Dark-ness be o-ver me, My rest a

me! Still all my song shall be, Near-er, my God, to thee, Near-er to thee!

stone, Yet in my dreams I'd be, Near-er, my God, to thee, Near-er to thee!

Hymn 769. **LYTE. 6s & 4s.** J. P. H.

1. Je - sus, thy name I love, All oth - er names a - bove, Je - sus, my Lord! Oh! thou art

2. Thou, bless-ed Son of God, Hast bought me with thy blood. Je - sus, my Lord! Oh! how great

all to me! Noth -ing to please I see, Noth - ing a - part from thee, Je - sus, my Lord!

is thy love, All oth - er loves a - bove, Love that I dai - ly prove, Je - sus, my Lord!

Hymn 773. **DUNCAN. 6s & 4s.** J. P. H.

1. Sav - iour! I fol - low on, Guid - ed by thee. See - ing not yet the hand That lead-eth me:

2. Riv - en the rock for me Thirst to re - lieve, Man - na from heav-en falls Fresh ev - ery eve;

Hushed be my heart and still, Fear I no further ill, On - ly to meet thy will My will shall be.

Nev - er a want se -vere Caus-eth my eye a tear, But thou dost whisper near, "On - ly be-lieve!"

EVENING PRAYER.

Rossini.

1. The day, the day is done! I thank thee, Lord, a - lone, 'Tis even - ing,

2. The day, the day is done! I bless thee, Might - y One, 'Tis even - ing,

and I cry, Sav - iour be nigh, Sav - iour be nigh,

and I cry, Sav - iour be nigh, Sav - iour be nigh; O hear my

Sav - iour be nigh: This night from sin me keep, Pre - serve me

even - ing cry: This night from ill me keep, Pre - serve me
Sav - iour be nigh:

while I sleep, O hear my even-ing cry, Dear Sav - iour, be thou nigh.

while I sleep, O hear my even-ing cry, Dear Sav - iour, be thou nigh.

THE LORD'S PRAYER.

J. P. HOLBROOK.

Our Fa - ther who art in heaven, Hal-lowed be thy name; Thy king-dom

Our Fa - ther who art in heaven, Hal-lowed be thy name; Thy king-dom

come, Thy will be done on earth, as it is in heaven. Give us this day

come, Thy will be done on earth, as it is in heaven. Give us this day

our dai - ly bread; and for-give us our tres - pass - es, As we for-

our dai - ly bread; and for-give us our tres - pass - es, As we for-

give them that tres - pass a - gainst us; And lead us not in - to tempt-a - tion,

give them that tres - pass a - gainst us; And lead us not in - to tempt-a - tion,

But de - liv - er us from e - vil; For thine is the king - dom, and the

cres.

But de - liv - er us from e - vil; For thine is the king - dom, and the

pow - er, and the glo - ry, For ev - er and ev - er. A - men.

pp

pow - er, and the glo - ry, For ev - er and ev - er. A - men.

Hymn from ZINZENDORF. **ZINZENDORF. 5s & 8s.** DRESE.

1. Je - su, day by day, Guide us on life's way; Nought of dan - gers will we reck - on,
2. Hard should seem our lot, Let us wa - ver not, Nev - er mur - mur at our cross - es,

3. When the heart must know Pain for oth - ers woe, When be - neath its own 'tis sink - ing,
4. Thus our path shall be Dai - ly traced by thee; Draw thou near - er when 'tis rough - er,

Sim - ply haste where thou dost beck - on; Lead us by the hand To our fa - ther - land.
In dark days of griefs and loss - es; 'Tis thro' tri - al we Here must pass to thee.

Give us pa - tience, hope un-shrink-ing, Fix our eyes, O Friend, On our jour - ney's end.
Help us most when most we suf - fer, And when all is o'er, Ope to us thy door.

Hymn 138. **SECOND CHURCH.** 7s. J. P. H.

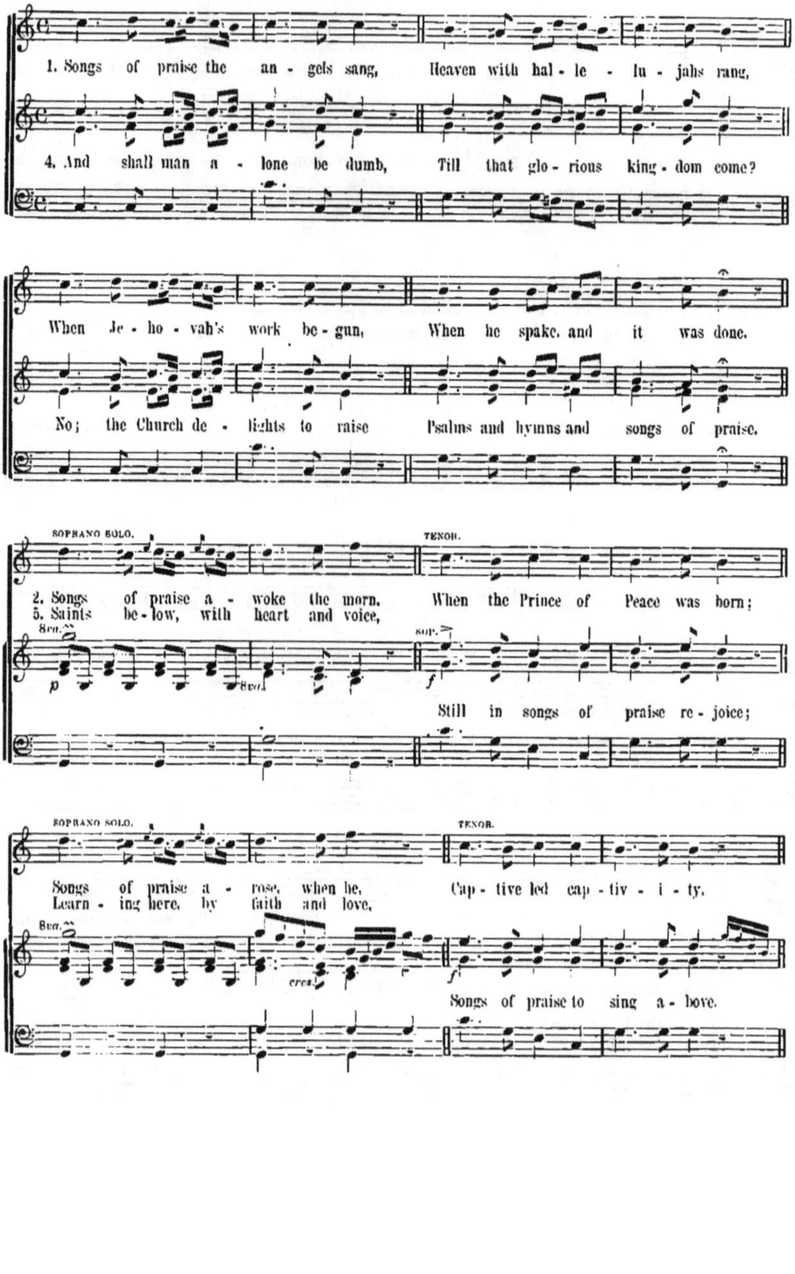

SECOND CHURCH. Concluded.

3. Heaven and earth must pass a - way— Songs of praise shall crown that day;

6. Borne up - on their lat - est breath Songs of praise shall con - quer death;

God will make new heavens and earth-- Songs of praise shall hail their birth.

Then, a - mid e - ter - nal joy, Songs of praise their powers em - ploy.

Hymn 630.   WINONA.   7's.   S. H. MORLIN.

1. Sovereign Rul - er of the skies, Ev - er gra - cious, ev - er wise.

4. O thou Gra - cious, Wise, and Just, In thy hands my life I trust;

All my times are in thy hand, All e - vents at thy com - mand.

Have I some - what dear - er still?— I re - sign it to thy will.

Hymn 606.   HASTINGS.   7s.   Concone.

1. Lord, thou art my rock of strength, And my home is in thine arms:

2. When my tri - als tar - ry long Un - to thee I look and wait;

Thou wilt send me help at length, And I feel no wild a - larms;

Know - ing none, though keen and strong, Can my trust in thee a - bate;

Sin nor death can pierce the shield Thy de - fence has o'er me thrown,

And this faith I long have nursed, Comes a - lone, O God, from thee;

Up to thee my - self I yield, And my sor - rows are thine own.

Thou my heart didst o - pen first, Thou didst set this hope in me.

Hymn 666.　　　**WELD.**　**7s.**　　　J. P. H.

1. Cast thy bur - den on the Lord, On - ly lean up - on his word;

2. He sus - tains thee by his hand, He en - a - bles thee to stand;

Thou wilt soon have cause to bless His un - chang - ing faith - ful - ness,

Those, whom Je - sus once hath loved, From his grace are nev - er moved.

Hymn 415.　　　**THOMAS.**　**7s.**　　　J. P. H.

1. Ho - ly Spir - it! gen - tly come, Raise us from our fall - en state;

2. Now thy quickening in - fluence bring, On our spir - its sweet - ly move;

Fix thy ev - er - last - ing home In the hearts thou didst cre - ate.

O - pen ev - ery mouth to sing Je - sus' ev - er - last - ing love.

Hymn 549. **MITCHELL.** 7s. Mercadante.

Andante, Soprano Solo.

1. Thou who didst on Cal - - vary bleed, Thou who
4. There on thee I cast my care, There to

dost for sin - - ners plead, Help me in my
thee I raise ..... my prayer, Je - - sus, save me

time of need, Je - - sus, Sav - iour, hear my cry!
from de - spair, Save me, save me, or I die!

3. Foes with - out and fears with - in, With no plea thy grace to win,
ril.

5. When the storms of tri - al lower, When I feel tempt - a - tion's power,

MITCHELL. Concluded.

But that thou canst save from sin, Je - sus, to thy cross I fly!

In the last and dark - est hour, Je - sus, Sav - iour, be thou nigh!

Hymn 838. **BURT. 7s.** Donizetti.

TENOR.

1. Chos - en not for good in me, Waked from com - ing wrath to flee,

SOPRANO.

2. Oft I walk be - neath the cloud, Dark as mid-night's gloom - y shroud;

Hid - den in the Sav - iour's side, By the Spir - it sanc - ti - fied—

But, when fear is at the height, Je - sus comes, and all is light;

Teach me, Lord, on earth to show, By my love, how much I owe.

Bless - ed Je - sus! bid me show Doubt - ing saints how much I owe.

Hymn 550.   BENSON.   7s.   VERDI.

Largo Cantabile.

1. Je - sus, Lamb of God, for me   Thou, the Lord of life, did-t die:

pp   *mf*

2. Nev - er bowed a mar-tyr's head   Weighed with e - qual sor - row down;

DUET—TENOR.

Whith - er whith-er 'but to thee,   Can a trem-bling sin - ner fly!

ritard.

SOPRANO.

Nev - er blood so rich was shed,   Nev - er king wore such a crown;

Death's dark wa - ters o'er me roll.   Save, oh, save my sink - ing soul!

cres.   *poco e poco.*   *f* *pp*   *rit.*

To thy cross and sac - ri - fice   Faith now lifts her tear - ful eyes.

Hymn 786.   HEYWOOD.   7s.   CONCONE.

1. Shep-herd, with thy tend - erest love,   Guide me to thy fold a - bove;

p   *p*

3. Je - sus, with thy pres - ence blest   Death is life, and la - bor rest;

HEYWOOD. Concluded.

Let me hear thy gen - tle voice; More and more in thee re - joice;

f

Guide me while I draw my breath, Guard me through the gate of death.

From thy full - ness grace re - ceive, Ev - er in thy Spir - it live.

p

And at last, oh, let me stand, With the sheep at thy right hand.

Hymn 461. **PARSONS. 7s.** J. P. H.

1. Would you win a soul to God? Tell him of a Sav - iour's blood,

2. Tell him — it was sov - ereign grace Led thee first to seek his face;

Once for dy - ing sin - ners spilt, To a - tone for all their guilt.

Made thee choose the bet - ter part, Wrought sal - va - tion in thy heart.

Hymn 612.   **CAMP.**   **7s.**   J. P. H.

1. When a - long life's thorn - y road, Faints the soul be - neath the load,

2. Thou, our Sav - iour, from the throne List - 'nest to thy peo - ple's moan;

By its cares and sins op - pressed, Finds on earth no peace or rest;

Thou, the liv - ing Head, dost share Ev - ery pang thy mem - bers bear;

When the wi - ly tempt - er's near, Fill - ing us with doubt and fear;

Full of ten - der - ness thou art, Thou wilt heal the bro - ken heart;

Je - sus, to thy feet we flee, Je - sus we will look to thee.

Full of power, thine arm shall quell All the rage and might of hell.

1. When our heads are bowed with woe; When our bit-ter tears o'er-flow;

2. When the heart is sad with-in, With the thought of all its sin;

When we mourn the lost, the dear, Je-sus, Son of Ma-ry, hear!

When the spir-it shrinks with fear, Je-sus, Son of Ma-ry, hear!

Thou our fee-ble flesh hast worn; Thou our mor-tal griefs hast borne;

Accelerando.

Thou the shame, the grief, hast known; Though the sins were not thine own,

rit.

Thou hast shed the hu-man tear: Je-sus, Son of Ma-ry, hear!

Thou hast deigned their load to bear: Je-sus, Son of Ma-ry, hear!

Hymn 319.   **CULBERTSON.** **7s.**   Wunderlich.

1. Go   to   dark   Geth - sem - a - ne,   Ye   that   feel   the   tempt - er's   power:

2. Fol - low   to   the   judg - ment - hall;   View   the   Lord   of   life   ar - raigned:

Your   Re - deem - er's   con - flict   see,   Watch   with   him   one   bit - ter   hour:

Oh,   the   worm - wood   and   the   gall! ....   Oh,   the   pangs   his   soul   sus - tained!

Turn   not   from   his   griefs   a - way,   Learn   of   Je - sus   Christ   to   pray.

Shun   not   suf - fering, shame,   or   loss;   Learn   of   him   to   bear   the   cross.

Hymn 415.   **BUDINGTON.** **7s.**   Arr.

Trio.

1. Ho - ly   Spir - it!   gen - tly   come,   Raise   us   from   our   fall - en   state.   Fix   thy   ev - er -

2. Now   thy   quickening   in - fluence bring,   On   our   spir - its   sweet - ly   move: O - pen   ev - ery

BUDINGTON. Concluded.

last - ing home In the hearts thou didst cre - ate; Fix thy ev - er - last - ing

mouth to sing Je - sus' ev - er - last - ing love; O - pen ev - ery mouth to

home In the hearts thou didst cre - ate, In the hearts thou didst cre - ate.

sing Je - sus' ev - er - last - ing love, Je - sus' ev - er - last - ing love.

Hymn 168. **WEBER.** 7's. Von Weber.

1. Soft - ly fades the twi - light ray..... Of the ho - ly Sab - bath day;

2. Night her sol - emn man - tle spreads O'er the earth as day - light fades;

Gen - tly as life's set - ting sun, When the Chris - tian's course is run.

All things tell of calm re - pose, At the ho - ly Sab - bath's close.

Hymn 605.   **REFUGE. 7s.**   J. P. H.

Andante.

1. Je - sus! lov - er of my soul, Let me to thy bo - som fly

2. Oth - er ref - uge have I none; Hangs my help - less soul on thee;

While the bil - lows near me roll, While the tem - pest still is high.

pp *rit.*

Leave, ah! leave me not a - lone. Still sup - port and com - fort me.

Hide me, 0 my Sav - iour! hide, Till the storm of life is past;

ff *pp*

All my trust on thee is stayed; All my help from thee I bring;

Safe in - to the ha - ven guide; Oh, re - ceive my soul at last!

f *p*

Cov - er my de - fence - less head With the shad - ow of thy wing.

Hymn 84.   **LOWELL.** **7's.**   J. P. H.

Duet. Tenor & Soprano.

1. Sweet the time, ex - ceed - ing sweet! When the saints to - geth - er meet,

mp

3. Sing the Son's a - maz - ing love; How he left the realms a - bove,

When the Sav - iour is the theme, When they joy to sing of him.

p

Took our na - ture and our place, Lived and died to save our race.

2. Sing we then e - ter - nal love, Such as did the Fa - ther move:

p

4. Sing we, too, the Spir - it's love; With our stub - born hearts he strove,

He be - held the world un - done, Loved the world, and gave his Son.

f   *p*

Filled our minds with grief and fear, Brought the pre - cious Sav - iour near.

Hymn 1149. PERRY. 7s. Arranged.

1. Hark! the song of Ju - bi - lee, Loud as might - y thun - ders roar,

2. Hal - le - lu - jah! hark, the sound, From the depths un - to the skies,

Or the full - ness of the sea, When it breaks up - on the shore!

Wakes a - bove, be - neath, a - round, All cre - a - tion's har - mo - nies!

Hal - le - lu - jah! for the Lord God om - nip - o - tent, shall reign!

See Je - ho - vah's ban - ner furled, Sheathed his sword, he speaks—'tis done!

Hal - le - lu - jah! let the word Ech - o round the earth and main.

And the king - doms of this world Are the king - doms of his Son!

Hymn 1151.   **STANLEY. 7s.**   Abt.

SOPRANO.

1. Watchman! tell us of the night, What its signs of prom-ise are.—
2. Watchman! tell us of the night, High-er yet that star as-cends.—

BASS OR TENOR.

Traveler! o'er yon mountain's height See that glo - ry-beaming star!
Traveler! bless - ed - ness and light, Peace and truth its course por - tends!

Watchman! does its beauteous ray Aught of joy or hope fore-tell?— Trav-eler! yes; it

Watchman! will its beams a - lone Gild the spot that gave them birth? Trav-eler! a - ges

CHORUS.

BASS.

brings the day— Prom - ised day of Is - ra - el, Prom - ised day of Is - ra - el.

are its own, See, it bursts o'er all the earth! See, it bursts o'er all the earth!

Hymn 838. **EARLE.** 7s. 6l. J. P. H

1. Chos - en not for good in me, Waked from com - ing wrath to flee,

2. Oft I walk be - neath the cloud, Dark as mid - night's gloom - y shroud;

Hid - den in the Sav - iour's side. By the Spir - it sanc - ti - fied—

But, when fear is at the height, Je - sus comes, and all is light;

Teach me, Lord, on earth to show, By my love, how much I owe.

Bless - ed Je - sus! bid me show Doubt - ing saints how much I owe.

Hymn 830. **REPOSE.** 7s. 6l. KÜCKEN.

1. Qui - et, Lord, my fro - ward heart, Make me teach - a - ble and mild,

2. What thou shalt to - day pro - vide, Let me as a child re - ceive;

REPOSE. **Concluded.**

Up - right, sim - ple, free from art, Make me as a wean - ed child:

What to - mor - row may be - tide, Calm - ly to thy wis - dom leave:

From dis - trust and en - vy free, Pleased with all that pleas - es thee.

'Tis e - nough that thou wilt care; Why should I the bur - den bear.

Hymn 836.   **COX.** **7s.**   J. P. H.

1. Je - sus, all - a - ton - ing Lamb, Thine, and on - ly thine, I am:

2. Thou my one thing need - ful be; Let me ev - er cleave to thee;

Take my bod - y, spir - it, soul: On - ly thou pos - sess the whole.

Let me choose the bet - ter part: Let me give thee all my heart.

Hymn 64.   **CAMPBELL. 7s.**   VERDI.

SOLO. TENOR OR SOPRANO.

1. In this calm im - press - ive hour, Let my prayer as - cend on high;
2. With the morn-ing's ear - ly ray, While the shades of night de - part,

ad lib.

portata.

God of mer - cy! God of power! Hear me, when to thee I cry:
Let thy beams of light con - vey Joy and glad - ness to my heart:

QUARTET.

God of mer - cy! God of power! Hear me, when to thee I cry:......

Let thy beams of light con - vey Joy and glad - ness to my heart:......

Hear me from thy loft - y throne, For the sake of Christ, thy Son.

rit.

Now o'er all my steps pre - side, And for all my wants pro - vide.

Hymn 272.   FORD.   7s.   BASSINI.

1. Ho - ly Fa - ther, hear my cry;   Ho - ly Sav - iour, bend thine ear;
3. Fa - ther, let me taste thy love;   Sav - iour, fill my soul with peace;

Ho - ly Spir - it, come thou nigh;...   Fa - ther, Sav - iour, Spir - it, hear!..
Spir - it, come my heart to move;...   Fa - ther, Son, and Spir - it, bless!..

2. Fa - ther, save me from my sin;.... Sav - iour, I thy mer - cy crave;
4. Fa - ther, Son, and Spir - it— thou.... One Je - ho - vah, shed a - broad

Gra - cious Spir - it, make me clean;   Fa - ther, Son, and Spir - it, save!
All thy grace with - in me now;   Be my Fa - ther and my God!

Hymn 786. **STANFORD.** 7s. J. P. H.

1. Shep - herd, with thy ten - derest love, Guide me to thy fold a - bove:

ritard.

2. Filled by thee my cup o'er - flows, For thy love no lim - it knows:

Let me hear thy gen - tle voice; More and more in thee re - joice;

p   *f cres.*

Guard - ian an - gels, ev - er nigh, Lead and draw my soul on high;

From thy full - ness grace re - ceive, Ev - er in thy Spir - it live.

mf   *ritard.*

Con - stant to my lat - est end, Thou my foot - steps wilt at - tend.

Words by E. ROWLAND SILL. **ROWLAND.** J. P. H.

1. Fa - ther in Heav - en! hum - bly be - fore thee, Kneel - ing in

2. God watch - ing o'er us, sleeps not nor slum - bers, Faith - ful night -

ROWLAND. Concluded.

prayer, thy child - ren ap - pear, We in our weak - ness, we in our

watch - es, his an - gels keep, Through all the dark - ness, un - to the

blind - ness, Thou in thy wis - dom, hear us, oh, hear.

dawn - ing, To his be - lov - ed he giv - eth sleep.

Hymn 836. LEEDS. 7s. HERZ.

1. Je - sus, all - a - ton - ing Lamb, Thine, and on - ly thine, I am:......

2. Thou my one thing need - ful be;.. Let me ev - er cleave to thee;.....

Take my bod - y, spir - it, soul; On - ly thou pos - sess the whole.

Let me choose the bet - ter part; Let me give thee all my heart.

Hymn 168.   **SANDS. 7s.**   J. P. H.

1. Soft - ly fades the twi - light ray   Of the ho - ly Sab - bath day;

4. Still the Spir - it lin - gers near,   Where the even - ing wor - ship - er

Gen - tly as life's set - ting sun,   When the Christian's course is run.

Seeks com - mun - ion with the skies,   Press - es on - ward to the prize.

2. Night her sol - emn man - tle spreads   O'er the earth as day - light fades;

5. Sav - iour! may our Sabbaths be   Days of joy and peace in thee,

All things tell of calm re - pose,   At the ho - ly Sabbath's close.

Till in heaven our souls re - pose,   Where the Sab - bath ne'er shall close.

Hymn 561.   OGDEN.   7s.   Bassini.

1. Je - sus, save my dy - ing soul; Make the bro - ken spir - it whole:

3. All my guilt to thee is known; Thou art right - eous, thou a - lone:

Hum - ble in the dust I lie: Sav - iour, leave me not to die.

All my help is from thy cross, All be - side I count but loss,

2. Je - sus, full of ev - ery grace, Now re - veal thy smil - ing face;

4. Lord, in thee I now be - lieve; Wilt thou, wilt thou not for - give?

Grant the joy of sin for - given, Fore - taste of the bliss of heaven.

Help - less at thy feet I lie; Sav - iour, leave me not to die.

Hymn 1006.   **LUQUER.   7s. 121.**   Mercadante.

Poco adagio.

1. When our heads are bowed with woe;   When our bit - ter tears o'er-flow;
D. C. When the heart is sad with - in,   With the thought of all its sin;

4. Thou the shame, the grief, hast known;   Though the sins were not thine own;
D. C. Thou hast bowed the dy - ing head;   Thou the blood of life hast shed;

Fine.

When we mourn the lost. the dear,   Je - sus, Son of Ma - ry, hear!
D. C. When the spir - it shrinks with fear,   Je - sus, Son of Ma - ry, hear!

Thou hast deigned their load to bear: Je - sus, Son of Ma - ry, hear!
D. C. Thou hast filled a mor - tal bier: Je - sus, Son of Ma - ry, hear!

2. Thou our fee - ble flesh hast worn;   Thou our mor - tal griefs hast borne;

5. When our eyes grow dim in death;   When we heave the part - ing breath;

D. C.

2. Thou hast shed the hu - man tear: Je - sus, Son of Ma - ry, hear!......
cres.   *rit.*   *f*

5. When our sol - emn doom is near,   Je - sus, Son of Ma - ry. hear!......

Hymn 422.   **EDMONDS. 7s.**   Monpou.

1. Come, di - vine and peace - ful Guest, En - ter each de - vot - ed breast;

Ho - ly Ghost, our hearts in - spire, Kin - dle there the Gos - pel fire.

2. Bid our sin and sor - row cease; Fill us with thy heaven - ly peace;

2. Bid our sin and sor - row cease; Fill us with thy heaven - ly peace;

Joy di - vine we then shall prove, Light of truth-- and fire of love.

Joy di - vine we then shall prove, Light of truth— and fire of love.

Hymn 786.   **AIKEN.**   **7s.**   MENDELSSOHN

Andante sostenuto.

1. Shep - herd with thy ten - derest love,   Guide me to thy fold a - bove;   Let me

2. Filled by thee my cup o'er - flows,   For thy love no lim - it knows: Guard - ian

hear thy gen - tle voice;   More and more in thee re - joice;   From thy full - ness grace re -

an - gels, ev - er nigh,   Lead and draw my soul on high;   Con - stant to my lat - est

ceive,   Ev - er in thy Spir - it live,....   Ev - er in thy Spir - it live.

end,   Thou my foot - steps wilt at - tend,....   Thou my foot - steps wilt at - tend.

Hymn 1229.   **DIX.**   **7s.**   German.

Repeat for 6 line verses.

1. Morn - ing breaks up - on the tomb,   Je - sus scat - ters all its gloom;

2. Ye, who are of death a - fraid,   Tri - umph in the scat - tered shade;

DIX. Concluded.

Day of tri - umph through the skies,-- See the glo - rious Sav - iour rise!

Drive your anx - ious cares a - way; See the place where Je - sus lay!

Words by HARRIET McEWEN KIMBALL. **KIMBALL. 8s & 6s.** J. P. H.

1. To Him who hears I whis - per all, And soft - lier than the
2. Wrapt in the peace that fol - lows prayer, I fold my hands in

3. No more life's mys - teries vex my thought, No cru - el doubts dis -

dews of heaven, The tears of Christ's com - pas - sion fall, I
per - fect trust, For - get - ful of the cross I bear, Through

- turb my breast. My heav - y la - den spir - it sought, And

know I am for - given, I know I am for - given.
noon - day heat and dust, Through noon - day heat and dust.

found the prom - ised rest, And found the prom - ised rest.

Hymn 1097.   **MIRIAM.   7s & 6s.**   J. P. H.

1. O Lamb of God! still keep me Near to thy wound-ed side; 'Tis on-ly there in

2. 'Tis on-ly in thee hid-ing, I feel my life se-cure— On-ly in thee a-

safe-ty And peace I can a-bide! What foes and snares sur-round me! What

bid-ing, The con-flict can en-dure: Thine arm the vic-to-ry gain-eth O'er

doubts and fears with-in! The grace that sought and found me, A-lone can keep me clean.

ev-ery hate-ful foe: Thy love my heart sus-tain-eth In all its care and woe.

Hymn 1286.   **MIRIAM. No. 2.   7s & 6s.**   J. P. H.

1. Je-ru-sa-lem, the glo-rious! The glo-ry of th' e-lect,— O dear and fu-ture

2. The Cross is all thy splen-dor, The cru-ci-fied, thy praise; His laud and ben-e-

MIRIAM. **No. 2.** **Concluded.**

vis - ion That ea - ger hearts ex - pect: Ev'n now by faith I see thee, Ev'n

dic - tion Thy ran - somed peo - ple raise;— Je - ru - sa - lem! ex - ult - ing On

here thy walls dis - cern; To thee my thoughts are kin - dled, And strive, and pant, and yearn!

that se - cur - est shore, I hope thee, wish thee, sing thee, And love thee ev - er - more!

Hymn 1002. **MARTH.** 7ᴺ & 5ᴺ. J. P. H.

1. In the dark and cloud - y day, When earth's rich - es flee a - way,

2. When the se - cret i - dol's gone That my poor heart yearned up - on,—

And the last hope will not stay, Sav - iour, com - fort me!......

Des - o - late, be - reft, a - lone, Sav - iour, com - fort me!......

Hymn 1096. **GERHARDT.** **7s & 6s.** J. P. H.

1. O sa - cred Head, now wound - ed, With grief and shame weighed down, Now scorn - ful - ly sur -

2. What thou, my Lord, hath suf - fered Was all for sin - ners' gain: Mine, mine was the trans -

round - ed With thorns, thine on - ly crown; O sa - cred Head, what glo - ry, What

gres - sion, But thine the dead - ly pain: Lo, here I fall, my Sav - iour! 'Tis

bliss, till now was thine! Yet, though des-pised and go - ry, I joy to call thee mine.

I de-serve thy place; Look on me with thy fa - vor, Vouch-safe to me thy grace.

Hymn 1288. **BERNARD.** **7s & 6s.** J. P. H.

1. For thee, O dear, dear Coun - try! Mine eyes their vig - ils keep: For ver - y love, be -

2. Thy age - less walls are bond - ed With am - e - thyst un - priced; The saints build up the

BERNARD. **Concluded.**

hold - ing Thy hap - py name, they weep ;-- O one, O on - ly man - sion ! O Par - a -

fab - ric. The cor - ner-stone is CHRIST ! Up - on the Rock of A - ges They raise thy

dise of joy ! Where tears are ev - er ban - ished, And bliss hath no al - loy.

ho - ly tower ; Thine is the vic - tor's lau - rel, And thine the gold - en dower.

Hymn 1223. **POMEROY.** **7s & 6s.** J. P. H.

1. No, no, it is not dy - ing To go un - to our God ; This gloom - y earth for - sak - ing,

2. No, no, it is not dy - ing Heaven's cit - i - zen to be ; A crown im - mor - tal wear - ing,

Our jour - ney homeward tak - ing, A - long the star - ry road, A - long the star - ry road.

And rest un - brok - en shar - ing, From care and con - flict free, From care and con - flict free.

Hymn 1116. **DENMAN.** 7s & 6s. J. P. H.

1. Lamb of God! whose bleed-ing love We now re-call to mind,

2. By thine ag-o-niz-ing pain, And blood-y sweat, we pray—

Send the an-swer from a-bove, And let us mer-cy find;

By thy dy-ing love to man, Take all...... our sins a-way:

Think on us, who think on thee, Ev-ery bur-dened soul re-lease;

Burst our bonds, and set us free, From all sin do thou re-lease;

Oh, re-mem-ber Cal-va-ry, And bid us go in peace!

Oh, re-mem-ber Cal-va-ry, And bid us go in peace!

Hymn 464.   COLEMAN.   7s & 6s.   J. P. H.

1. Droop - ing souls, no long - er mourn, Je - sus still is pre - - cious;

2. He has par - dons full and free, Droop - ing souls to glad - - den;

mf

If to him you now re - turn, Heaven will be pro - pi - - tious;

Still he cries—"Come un - to me, Wea - ry, heav - y lad - - en!"

Je - sus now is pass - ing by, Call - ing wan - derers near him;

Though your sins like mount - ains high, Rise, and reach to heav - en,

Droop - ing souls you need not die, Go to him and hear him!

Soon as you on him re - ly, All shall be for - giv - en.

Hymn 554. **BARNES.** 7s & 6s. ABT.

1. We stand in deep re-pent-ance, Be-fore thy throne of love;
2. Oh! shouldst thou from us fall-en With-hold thy grace to guide,

O God of grace, for-give us; The stain of guilt re-move;
For-ev-er we should wan-der. From thee, and peace, a-side:

The stain of guilt re-move; Be-hold us while with weep-ing
Be-hold
From thee, and peace, a-side; But thou to spir-its con-trite
But thou

We lift our eyes to thee; And all our sins sub-du-ing, And
dim.   cres.
Dost light and life im-part, That man may learn to serve thee. That
And all
That man

BARNES. Concluded.

all our sins sub-du-ing, Our Fa-ther, set us free! Our Fa-ther, set us free!

man may learn to serve thee With thank-ful, joy-ous heart, With thank-ful, joy-ous heart.

Hymn 1308.   **EWING.   7s & 6s.**   Bp. Ewing.

1. There is a land im-mor-tal, The beau-ti-ful of lands; Be-side its an-cient

2. Though dark and drear the pas-sage That lead-eth to the gate. Yet grace comes with the

port-al A si-lent sen-try stands; He on-ly can un-do it, And

mes-sage, To souls that watch and wait; And at the time ap-point-ed A

o-pen wide the door; And mor-tals who pass through it, Are mor-tals nev-er-more.

mes-sen-ger comes down, And leads the Lord's a-noint-ed From cross to glo-ry's crown.

140

Hymn 419. **SCUDDER.** 7s, 6s & 8s. Langer

1. Bless-ed Com-fort-er, come down, And live and move in me: Make my ev-ery

2. Let me in thy love re-joice, Thy shrine, thy pure a-bode: Tell me, by thine

rit.

deed thy own, In all things led by thee; Bid my ev-ery lust de-part.

in-ward voice, I am a child of God: Lord, I choose the bet-ter part,

p

And now with me, vouch-safe to dwell, Faith-ful Wit-ness, in my heart Thy per-fect

Je-sus, I wait thy peace to feel; Send the wit-ness, in my heart The Ho-ly

rit. *p*

love re-veal; Faith-ful Wit-ness, in my heart Thy per-fect love re-veal.

Ghost re-veal; Send the wit-ness, in my heart The Ho-ly Ghost re-veal.

rit.

Hymn 620.   **BRANNAN.**   **7s, 6s & 8s.**   J. P. H.

1. Thou, O Lord, in ten - der love, Dost all my bur - dens bear;

2. Care - ful with - out care I am, Nor feel my hap - py toil!

Lift my heart to things a - bove, And fix it ev - er there!

Kept in peace by Je - sus' name, Sup - port - ed by his smile.

Calm in tu - mult's whirl I sit, 'Midst bus - y mul - ti - tudes a - lone;

Joy - ful thus my faith to show, I find his ser - vice my re - ward;

Sweet - ly wait - ing at thy feet, Till all thy will be done.

Ev - ery work I do be - low, I do it to the Lord.

Hymn 132. HANSON. 7s & 6s. J. P. H.

1. Praise the Lord, who reigns a - bove, And keeps his courts be - low;

2. Pub - lish, spread to all a - round The great Im - man - uel's name;

Praise him for his bound - less love, And all his great - ness show!

 rit.

Let the gos - pel trum - pet sound, The Prince of peace pro - claim!

TENOR SOLO.

Praise him for...... his no - ble deeds;.... Praise him for...... his match - less

Praise him, ev - - ery tune-ful string;.... All the reach.... of heaven - ly

One..

power;

art,

SOP. SOLO.

cres.

Him, from whom all good pro - ceeds,.... Let earth.... and heaven a - dore,

All the power of mu - sic bring,.... The mu - - sic of the heart,

rit.

HANSON. Concluded.

Him, from whom all good pro-ceeds, Let earth and heaven a-dore.

All the power of mu-sic bring, The mu-sic of the heart.

Hymn 125. **BARROWS.** **8s & 7s.** Arr. Monk.

1. Praise the Lord! ye heavens, a-dore him, Praise him, an-gels in the height;

3. Praise the Lord—for he is glo-rious; Nev-er shall his prom-ise fail;

Sun and moon, re-joice be-fore him; Praise him, all ye stars of light!

God hath made his saints vic-to-rious, Sin and death shall not pre-vail.

2. (Praise the Lord—for he hath spo-ken; Worlds his might-y voice o-beyed;)
(Laws which nev-er shall be bro-ken, For their guid-ance he hath made.)

4. (Praise the God of our sal-va-tion, Hosts on high his power pro-claim;)
(Heaven and earth, and all cre-a-tion, Laud and mag-ni-fy his name.)

SEAVER. 8s & 7s. J. P. H.

Hymn 1306 with Dox. 14.

Maestso.   *Small notes for third verse.*

1. Je - sus, bless - ed Me - di - a - tor! Thou the air - y path hast trod;

3. Lo! it comes, that day of won - der! Loud - er cho - rals shake the skies;

Thou the Judge, the Con - sum - ma - tor! Shep - herd of the fold of God!

Ha - des' gates are burst a - sun - der; See! the new - clothed myr - iads rise!

Can I trust a fel - low be - ing? Can I trust an an - gel's care?

Duet.p

Thought! re - press thy weak en - deav - or; Here must rea - son pros - trate fall;

O thou mer - ci - ful All - see - ing! Beam a - round my spir - it there.

Cho. ff

Oh, th'in - ef - fa - ble For - ev - er! And th'e - ter - nal All in All!

2. Bless-ed fold! no foe can en-ter; And no friend de-part-eth thence;

DUET.

DOX. 14. Praise the God of all cre-a-tion; Praise the Fa-ther's bound-less love:

Je-sus is their sun, their cen-tre, And their shield Om-nip-o-tence!

CHO. *ff*

Praise the Lamb, our ex-pi-a-tion, Priest and King en-throned a-bove:

Bless-ed, for the Lamb shall feed them, All their tears shall wipe a-way,

pp

Praise the Fount-ain of sal-va-tion, Him by whom our spir-its live:

To the liv-ing foun-tains lead them, Till fru-i-tion's per-fect day.

Un-di-vid-ed ad-o-ra-tion To the one Je-ho-vah give.

Hymn 270.   **WARNER.**   **8s & 7s.**   F. Otto.

1. God is love; his mer-cy bright-ens All the path in which we rove;

1. God is love; his mer-cy bright-ens All the path in which we rove;

Bliss he wakes and woe he light-ens; God is wis-dom. God is love,

cres.

Bliss he wakes and woe he light-ens; God is wis-dom. God is love,

God is wis-dom, God is love. 2. Chance and change are bus-y ev-er;

pp

God is wis-dom, God is love. 3. Ev'n the hour that dark-est seem-eth,

2. Man de-cays, and a-ges move; But his mer-cy wan-eth nev-er;
3. Will his change - less good-ness prove;

2. Man de-cays, and a-ges move;
3. Will his changeless goodness prove; From the gloom his brightness streameth,

WARNER. Concluded.

God is wis - dom, God is love, God is wis - dom, God is love.....

God is wis - dom, God is love, God is wis - dom, God is love.....

4. He with earth - ly cares en - twin - eth Hope and com - fort from a - bove:

4. He with earth - ly cares en - twin - eth Hope and com - fort from a - bove:

Ev - ery - where his glo - ry shin - eth; God is wis - dom, God is love,

Ev - ery - where his glo - ry shin - eth; God is wis - dom, God is love,

God is wis - dom, God is love..................................

God is wis - dom, God is love, is love, is love.

Hymn 288.　　　**SMITH.**　**8s & 7s.**　　　Himmel.

Andante.

1. Hark! what mean those ho - ly voic - es, Sweet - ly sound-ing through the skies?

3. "Peace on earth, good-will from heav - en, Reach-ing far as man is found;

Lo! th' an - gel - ic host re - joic - es; Heaven - ly hal - le - lu - jahs rise.

Souls re - deemed, and sins for - giv - en! Loud our gold - en harps shall sound.

2. Hear them tell the won - drous sto - ry, Hear them chant in hymns of joy:—

p cres. poco e poco.

4. "Christ is born, the great A - noint - ed; Heaven and earth his prais - es sing!

"Glo - ry in the high - est, glo - ry! Glo - ry be to God most high!

f

Oh, re - ceive whom God ap - point - ed, For your Proph - et, Priest, and King!

Hymn 186. **SHEPARD.** **8s & 7s.** BEETHOVEN.

1. Heaven-ly Fa-ther, grant thy bless-ing On the teach-ing of this day;

2. Have we wan-dered? oh, for-give us; Have we wished from truth to rove?

That our hearts, thy fear pos-sess-ing, May from sin be turned a-way.

Turn, oh, turn us, and re-ceive us, And in-cline us thee to love.

Hymn 551. **BULLARD.** **8s & 7s.** FLOTOW.

1. La-bor-ing and heav-y lad-en, With my sins, O Lord I roam,

2. Make my stub-born spir-it will-ing To o-bey thy gra-cious voice,

While I know thou hast in-vit-ed All such wan-der-ers to their home.

At the cross to leave its bur-den, And de-part-ing to re-joice.

Hymn 266. **TILTON.** **8s & 7s.** Oesten.

1. Lord, with glow - ing heart I'd praise thee For the bliss thy love be - stows;

2. Praise, my soul, the God that sought thee, Wretch - ed wan - d'rer, far a - stray;

For the pardoning grace that saves me, And the peace that from it flows:

Found thee lost, and kind - ly brought thee From the paths of death a - way;

Help, O God, my weak en - deav - or; This dull soul to rap - - ture raise;

Praise, with love's de - vout - est feel - ing, Him who saw thy guilt - born fear,

Thou must light the flame, or nev - er Can my love be warmed to praise.

And, the light of hope re - veal - ing, Bade the blood - stained cross ap - pear.

Hymn 265.　　　**CARLTON.**　**8s & 7s.**　　Concone.

1. Lord, thy glo - ry fills the heav - en; Earth is with its full - ness stored;

2. Ev - er thus in God's high prais - es, Breth - ren, let our tongues u - nite.

Un - to thee be glo - ry giv - en, Ho - ly, ho - ly, ho - ly Lord!

While our thoughts his great - ness rais - es, And our love his gifts ex - cite:

Heaven is still with an - thems ring - ing; Earth takes up the an - gels' cry,

With his ser - aph train be - fore him, With his ho - ly church be - low,

Ho - ly, ho - ly, ho - ly, sing - ing, Lord of hosts, thou Lord most high.

Thus u - nite we to a - dore him, Bid we thus our an - them flow.

Hymn 179.   **WORTHINGTON.** 8s & 7s.   BAYLEY.

1. Sav - iour, breathe an even - ing bless - ing, Ere re - pose our spir - its seal;

3, Though the night be dark and drear - y, Dark - ness can - not hide from thee;

Sin and want we come con - fess - ing; Thou canst save, and thou canst heal.

Thou art he who, nev - er wea - ry, Watch - eth where thy peo - ple be.

2. Though de - struc - tion walk a - round us, Though the ar - row near us fly,

4, Should swift death this night o'er - take us, And our couch be - come our tomb,

An - - gel guards from thee sur - round us; We are safe if thou art
May..... the morn in heaven a - wake us, Clad in light and death - less
An - gel guards, an - gel guards
May the morn, may the morn

An - gel guards from thee.... sur - round us; We are safe if thou art
May the morn in heaven.. a - wake us, Clad in light and death - less

An - gel guards from thee sur - round us;
May the morn in heaven a - wake us,

WORTHINGTON. Concluded.

nigh, We are safe if thou art nigh, We are safe if thou art nigh,
bloom, Clad in light and deathless bloom, Clad in light and death - less bloom.

p *rit.* *pp*

thou art nigh, We are safe if thou art nigh.
death - less bloom, Clad in light and death - less bloom.

Hymn 266. **HOGARTH.** **8s & 7s.** SCHUBERT.

1. (Lord, with glow - ing heart I'd praise thee For the bliss thy love be - stows;)
   (For the pardon - ing grace that saves me, And the peace that from it flows;)

2. (Praise, my soul, the God that sought thee, Wretch - ed wan - d'rer, far a - stray;)
   (Found thee lost, and kind - ly brought thee From the paths of death a - way;)

Help, O God, my weak en - deav - or: This dull soul to rap - ture raise:
cres.
Praise, with love's de - vout - est feel - ing, Him who saw thy guilt - born fear,

Thou must light the flame, or nev - er Can my love be warmed to praise.
cres.
And, the light of hope re - veal - ing, Bade the blood - stained cross ap - pear.

Hymn 617. **GAYLORD.** **8s & 7s.** Arranged.

1. Take me, O my Fa-ther, take me! Take me, save me, through thy Son;

2. Fruit-less years with grief re-call-ing, Hum-bly I con-fess my sin;

That which thou wouldst have me, make me, Let thy will in me be done.

D. S. Wea-ry come I now, and pray-ing— Take me to thy love, my God!

At thy feet, O Fa-ther, fall-ing, To thy house-hold take me in.

D. S. Free-ly life and soul I of-fer— Gift un-wor-thy love like thine.

Long from thee my foot-steps stray-ing, Thorn-y proved the way I trod;

Free-ly now to thee I prof-fer This re-lent-ing heart of mine;

Hymn 760. **BAYLEY.** **8s & 7s.** BAYLEY.

1. Love di-vine, all love ex-cel-ling,-- Joy of heaven, to earth come down!

2. Breathe, oh, breathe thy lov-ing Spir-it In-to ev-ery troub-led breast!

BAYLEY. Concluded.

Fine.

Fix in us thy hum-ble dwell-ing, All thy faith-ful mer-cies crown;
D. S. Vis-it us with thy sal-va-tion, En-ter ev-ery trem-bling heart.

Let us all in thee in-her-it, Let us find thy prom-ised rest;
D. S. Speed-i-ly re-turn, and nev-er, Nev-er more thy tem-ples leave!

D. S.

Je-sus! thou art all com-pas-sion, Pure, un-bound-ed love thou art;

Come, al-might-y to de-liv-er, Let us all thy life re-ceive!

Hymn 1299. **OSBORNE.** 8s & 7s. GLUCK.

Andante.

1. This is not my place of rest-ing,—Mine's a cit-y yet to come; On-ward to it I am

2. In it all is light and glo-ry; O'er it shines a night-less day; Ev-ery trace of sin's sad

hast-ing— On to my e-ter-nal home, On to my e-ter-nal home.

sto-ry, All the curse, hath passed a-way, All the curse, hath passed a-way.

Hymn 1160. **STOUGHTON. 8s & 7s.** J. P. H.

1. Glo - rious things of thee are spok - en, Zi - on, cit - y of our God!

2. See, the streams of liv - ing wa - ters, Spring - ing from e - ter - nal love,

8:   *Fine*

He whose word can - not be brok - en, Formed thee for his own a - bode:
D. S. With sal - va - tion's walls sur - round - ed, Thou may'st smile at all thy foes.

Well sup - ply thy sons and daugh - ters, And all fear of want re - move:
D. S. Grace, which, like the Lord, the giv - er, Nev - er fails from age to age.

D. S. 8:

On the Rock of A - ges found - ed— What can shake thy sure re - pose?

Who can faint, while such a riv - er Ev - er flows their thirst t' as - suage?

GOODWIN. 8s & 7s. M. Haydn. Arr. by Monk.

1. Praise, my soul, the King of Heav - en, To his feet thy trib - ute bring;
2. Praise him for his grace and fa - vor To our fa - thers in dis - tress;

3. Fa - ther - like, he tends and spares us, Well our fee - ble frame he knows;
4. An - gels in the height a - dore him! Ye be - hold him face to face;

GOODWIN. Concluded.

Ran - somed, healed, res - tored, for - giv - en.
Praise him still the same as ev - er,

Ev - er - more his prais - es sing,
Slow to chide, and swift to bless ;

In his hands he gen - tly bears us,
Saints tri - umph - ant bow be - fore him!

Res - cues us from all our foes,
Gath - ered in from ev - ery race ;

Al - le - lu - ia! Al - le - lu - ia!
Al - le - lu - ia! Al - le - lu - ia!

Praise the ev - er - last - ing King.
Glo - rious in his faith - ful - ness.

Al - le - lu - ia! Al - le - lu - ia!
Al - le - lu - ia! Al - le - lu - ia!

Wide - ly yet his mer - cy flows.
Praise with us the God of grace.

Hymn 1299. **MILLER.** 8s & 7s. CHERUBINI

1. This is not my place of rest - ing,— Mine's a cit - y yet to come;
2. In it all is light and glo - ry; O'er it shines a night - less day ;

On - ward to it I am hast - ing— On to my e - ter - nal home,
Ev - ery trace of sin's sad sto - ry, All the curse, hath passed a - way.

Hymn 175.   **TRISTE.**   **8s & 7s.**   J. P. H.

1. Gen - tly, Lord, oh, gen - tly lead us   Through this lone - ly vale of tears;

3. In the hour of pain and an - guish,   In the hour when death draws near,

Through the chan - ges thou'st de - creed us,   Till our last great change ap - pears.

D. S. Let thy good - ness nev - er fail us,   Lead us in thy per - fect way.

Suf - fer not our hearts to lan - guish,—   Suf - fer not our souls to fear.

D. S. Till by an - gel - bands at - tend - ed,   We a - wake a - mong the blest.

2. When tempt - a - tion's darts as - sail us,   When in de - vious paths we stray,

4. And when mor - tal life is end - ed,   Bid us on thy bo - som rest,

Hymn 189.   **NOYES.**   **8s 7s & 4s.**   Monk.

1. While we low - ly bow be - fore thee,   Wilt thou, gra - cious Sav - iour, hear?

2. Fill us with thy Ho - ly Spir - it :   Sanc - ti - fy us by thy grace;

NOYES. Concluded.

We are poor and need - y sin - ners, Full of doubt and full of fear;

Oh, in - cline us more to love thee. And in dust our souls a - base.

Gra - cious Sav - iour, Gra - cious Sav - iour, Make us hum - ble and sin - cere.

Hear us, Sav - iour, Hear us, Sav - iour, And un - vail thy glo - rious face.

Hymn 671. **WESTMINISTER.** 8s & 7s. J. P. H.

1. On - ward, Chris - tian, though the re - gion Where thou art be drear and lone;

2. List - en, Chris - tian; their ho - san - na Roll - eth o'er thee: "God is love,"

God has set a guard - ian le - gion Ver - y near thee; press thou on.

Write up - on thy red - cross ban - ner, "Up - ward ev - er; heaven's a - bove."

Hymn 1306.   **HALLETT.**   **8s & 7s.**   Mozart.

1. Je - sus, bless - ed Me - di - a - tor! Thou the air - y path hast trod;

2. Bless - ed fold! no foe can en - ter; And no friend de - part - eth thence;

Thou the Judge, the Con-sum-ma - tor! Shep-herd of the fold of God! Can I trust a

Je - sus is their sun, their cen - tre, And their shield Om - nip - o - tence! Bless - ed, for the

fel - low - be - ing? Can I trust an an - gel's care? O thou mer - ci -

Lamb shall feed them, All their tears shall wipe a - way, To the liv - ing

ful All - see - ing! Beam a - round my spir - it there, Beam a - round my spir - it there.

fountains lead them, Till fru - i - tion's per - fect day, Till fru - i - tion's per - fect day.

Hymn 322.　　　**BUTLER.**　8s, 7s & 4s.　　　J. P. H.

1. Hark! the voice of love and mer - cy Sounds a - loud from Cal - va - ry;

2. "It is fin - ished!"—oh, what pleas - ure Do these charm - ing words af - ford!

3. Tune your harps a - new, ye ser - aphs! Join to sing the pleas - ing theme:

f　　　　　　　　　*ff*　　　　*p*

See!— it rends the rocks a - sun - der— Shakes the earth— and vails the sky:

Heaven - ly bless - ings, with - out meas - ure, Flow to us through Christ the Lord:

All in earth and heaven u - nit - ing, See 2nd ending for third verse.

"It is fin - ished!— It is fin - ished!"—Hear the dy - ing Sav - iour cry.

"It is fin - ished!— It is fin - ished!"—Saints! the dy - ing words re - cord.

2nd ending for third verse.　　　　　　　　　*p*

Join to praise Im - manuel's name: Hal - le - lu - jah!—Hal - le - lu - jah!— Glo - ry to the bleed - ing Lamb!

Unison.

Join to praise Im - manuel's name: Hal - le - lu - jah!—Hal - le - lu - jah!— Glo - ry to the bleed - ing Lamb!

Hymn 176. **NELSON.** 8s, 7s & 4s. J. P. H.

1. Guide me, O thou great Je - ho - vah, Pil - grim through this bar - ren land;

2. O - pen thou the crys - tal fount - ain Whence the heal - ing streams do flow;

I am weak, but thou art might y; Hold me with thou power - ful hand;

Let the fi - ery, cloud - y pil - lar Lead me all my jour - ney through;

Bread of heav - en, Bread of heav - en, Feed me till I want no more.

Strong De - liv - erer, Strong De - liv - erer, Be thou still my Strength and Shield.

Hymn 176. **SEGUR.** 8s, 7s & 4s. J. P. H.

1. Guide me, O thou great Je - ho - vah, Pil - grim through this bar - ren land;

2. O - pen thou the crys - tal fount - ain Whence the heal - ing streams do flow;

SEGUR. Concluded.

I am weak, but thou art might - y; Hold me with thy power - ful hand;

Let the fi - ery, cloud - y pil - lar Lead me all my jour - ney through;

Bread of heav - en, Bread of heav - en, Feed me till I want no more.

Strong De - liv - erer, Strong De - liv - erer, Be thou still my Strength and Shield.

Hymn 549.   **SAYRE.** 7s.   REDHEAD.

1. Thou who didst on Cal - vary bleed, Thou who dost for sin - ners plead,

2. In my dark - ness and my grief, With my heart of un - be - lief,

Help me in my time of need, Je - sus, Sav - iour, hear my cry!

I, who am of sin - ners chief, Je - sus, lift to thee mine eye!

Hymn 448. **STETSON.** 8s, 7s & 4s. HANDEL.

1. See, from Zi - on's sa - cred mountain, Streams of liv - ing wa - ter flow;

2. Through ten thou - sand chan - nels flow - ing, Streams of mer - cy find their way:

God has o - pened there a fount-ain, That sup - plies the world be - low:

Life, and health, and joy be - stow - ing, Wak - ing beau - ty from de - cay;

They are blessed, They are blessed, Who its sov - ereign vir - tues know.

O ye nations! O ye nations! Hail the long ex - pect - ed day.

Hymn 88. **CLARK.** 8s, 7s & 4s. ABT.

1. God is in his ho - ly tem - ple; All the earth keep si - lence here;

2. God in Christ re - veals his pres - ence, Throned up - on the mer - cy seat;

2

CLARK. Concluded.

Wor - ship him in truth and spir - it; Rev - erence him with god - ly fear;

Saints, re - joice, and sin - ners, trem - ble; Each pre - pare his God to meet:

Ho - ly, ho - ly, Ho - ly. ho - ly, Lord of hosts, our God, ap - pear!

Low - ly, low - ly, Low - ly, low - ly Bow, a - dor - ing at his feet.

Hymn 380. ORMOND. 7s. Monk.

1, Hail the day that sees him rise, Glo - rious to his na - tive skies!

2. There the glo - rious tri - umph waits; Lift your heads, e - ter - nal gates!

Christ, a - while to mor - tals given, En - ters now the gates of heaven.

Christ hath vanquished death and sin; Take the King of glo - ry in.

Hymn 189.   **PALMER.**   **8s,7s & 4s.**   H.

1. While we low - ly bow be - fore thee, Wilt thou, gra - cious Sav - iour, hear?

2. Fill us with thy Ho - ly Spir - it; Sanc - ti - fy us by thy grace;

We are poor and need - y sin - ners, Full of doubt and full of fear;

Oh, in - cline us more to love thee, And in dust our souls a - base.

Gra - cious Sav - iour, Gra - cious Sav - iour, Make us hum - ble and sin - cere.

Hear us, Sav - iour, Hear us, Sav - iour, And un - vail thy glo - rious face.

Hymn 1164.   **PROCTOR.**   **8s, 7s & 4s.**   J. P. H.

1. Songs a - new of hon - or fram - ing, Sing ye to the Lord a - lone;

2. Now he bids his great sal - va - tion Through the hea - then lands be told;

PROCTOR. Concluded.

All his won - drous works pro - claim - ing,— Je - sus won - drous works hath done!

Spread the news thro' ev - ery na - tion, And his acts of grace un - fold;

Glo - rious vic - tory, Glo - rious vic - tory His right hand and arm have won.

All the hea - then, All the hea - then Shall his right - eous - ness be - hold.

Hymn 1340.   **HALL. P. M.**   J. P. H.

1. Star of peace! to wan - derers wea - ry, Bright the beams that smile on me,

2. Star of hope! gleam on the bil - low, Bless the soul that sighs for thee;

Cheer the pi - lot's vis - ion drear - y, Far, far, far at sea, Far, far, far at sea.

Bless the sail - or's lone - ly pil - low, Far, far, far at sea, Far, far, far at sea.

Hymn 688.   **STORRS.**   9s & 8s.   J. P. Holbrook.

1. Chris - tian, the morn breaks sweet-ly o'er thee,   And all the mid - night shad-ows flee,

2. Tossed on time's rude, re - lent - less sur - ges,   Calm - ly composed, and daunt-less stand,

Tinged are the dis - tant skies with glo - ry,   A bea - con light hung out for thee;

For lo! be-yond those scenes e - mer - ges   The height that bounds the prom-ised land;

Chorus.

A - rise, a - rise! the light breaks o'er thee;   Thy name is grav - en on the throne;

Be - hold! be - hold! the land is near - ing,   Where the wild sea-storm's rage is o'er;

Thy home is in the world of glo - ry,   Where thy Re - deem - er reigns a - lone.

Hark! how the heavenly hosts are cheer - ing,   See in what throngs they range the shore!

Hymn 789.　　　**HOWE.　11s & 10s.**　　Arranged.

1. We would see Je - sus— for the shad - ows length - en

2. We would see Je - sus— the great Rock Foun - da - tion,

A - cross this lit - tle land - scape of our life: We would see Je - sus

Where - on our feet were set by sov - ereign grace; Not life, nor death, with

our weak faith to strength - en, For the last wea - ri -

all their ag - i - ta - tion, Can thence re - move...... us,

ness— the fi - nal strife. For the last wea - ri - ness— the fi - nal strife.

if we see his face. Can thence re - move... us, if we see his face.

Hymn 1120. **CROSBY. 11s.** J. P. H.

1. O gar - den of Ol - ives, thou dear honored spot, The fame of thy

2. Come, saints, and a - dore him; come, bow at his feet: Oh, give him the

won - ders shall ne'er be for - got; The theme most trans - port - ing to

glo - ry, the praise that is meet: Let joy - ful ho - san - nas un -

ser - aphs a - bove; The tri - umph of sor - row,—the tri - umph of love!

ceas - ing a - rise, And join the full cho - rus that glad - dens the skies!

Hymn 785. **BERLIN. 10s.** Mendelssohn, arr. by Goss.

1. A - bide with me! Fast falls the e - ven - tide, The dark - ness

2. Swift to its close ebbs out life's lit - tle day; Earth's joys grow

BERLIN. Concluded.

deep - ens— Lord, with me a - bide! When oth - er help - ers

dim, its glo - ries pass a - way; Change and de - cay in

fail, and comforts flee, Help of the help - less, oh, a - bide with me!

all a - round I see; O thou, who chang - est not, a - bide with me!

Hymn 924. **MURRAY. 11s.** J. P. H.

1. I once was a stran - ger to grace and to God; I knew not my

dan - ger, and felt not my load; Though friends spoke in rap - ture of

Christ on the tree, Je - ho - vah, my Sav - iour, seemed noth - ing to me.

Hymn 135.   KENDALL.   11s & 12s.   Mozart.

1. Oh,.... join ye the an - thems of tri - umph that rise

2. He .... gave to the light its be - nef - i - cent wings;

From the throng of the blest, from the hosts of the skies;

He con - troll - eth the coun - cils of.... sen - ates and kings;

Solo. Soprano.

Al - le - lu - ia, they sing, in rapt - - ur - ous strains,
From his throne in the clouds the light - - nings are hurled,

Al - le - lu - ia, the Lord God om - nip - o - tent reigns!
And he rul - eth the fac - tions that rage through the world;

KENDALL. Concluded.

Al - le - lu - ia, they sing, in rapt - ur - ous strains,

From his throne in the clouds the light - nings are hurled,

Al - le - lu - ia, the Lord God om - nip - o - tent reigns!

rit.

And he rul - eth the fac - tions that rage through the world;

Hymn from GERHARDT.

EDDY. 8s & 6s.

EBELING. 1677.

1. All my heart this night re - joi - ces, As I hear, Far and near, Sweet-est an - gel voic - es;
2. Hark! a voice from yon-der man - ger, Soft and sweet, Doth en- treat, "Flee from woe and dan - ger;

3. Hith - er come, ye heav-y - heart-ed, Who for sin, Deep with-in, Long and sore have smart-ed;
4. Hith - er come, ye poor and wretched, Know his will, Is to fill, Ev - ery hand out-stretch-ed;

"Christ is born," their choirs are sing - ing Till the air Ev - ery-where Now with joy is ring - ing.
Breth - ren, come, from all doth grieve you You are freed, All you need I will sure - ly give you."

For the poisoned wounds you're feel - ing, Help is near, One is here Might - y for their heal - ing!
Here are rich - es with-out meas - ure, Here for - get All re - gret, Fill your hearts with treas-ure.

Hymn 285.　　　**BROWN.**　**11s & 10s.**

Aut. Arr. by D. R. Stanford.

1. Brightest and best of the sons of the morn-ing! Dawn on our dark-ness, and
3. Say shall we yield him, in cost-ly de-vo-tion, O-dors of E-dom, and

lend us thine aid; Star of the East, the ho-ri-zon a-dorn-ing,
off'-rings di-vine? Gems of the mount-ain, and pearls of the o-cean,

Guide where our iu-fant Re-deem-er is laid. 2. Cold on his cra-dle the
Cold..... the
Myrrh from the for-est, or gold from the mine? 4. Vain-ly we of-fer each
Of-fer each

dew-drops are shin-ing; Low lies his head with the beasts of the stall!
Low with the,
am-ple ob-la-tion, Vain-ly with gold would his fa-vors se-cure:
Vain-ly his,

BROWN. Concluded.

An-gels a-dore him, in slum-ber re-clin-ing, Mak-er, and Mon-arch, and

mf cres. *f* *ritard.*

Rich-er by far, is the hearts ad-o-ra-tion; Dear-er to God are the

Sav-iour of all! Mak-er, and Mon-arch, and Sav-iour of all!

prayers of the poor. Dear-er to God are the prayers of the poor.

Hymn 1225. **MONTGOMERY.** 8s & 4s. LACHNER.

1. There is a calm for those who weep, A rest for wea-ry

2. The storm that racks the win-try sky No more dis-turbs their

pil-grims found; They soft-ly lie, and sweet-ly sleep, Low in the ground.

deep re-pose Than sum-mer eve-ning's lat-est sigh, That shuts the rose.

Hymn 138. **SONGS OF PRAISE.** 7s. J. P. H.

1. Songs of praise the an - gels sang, Heaven with hal - le - lu - jahs rang, When Je - ho - vah's

1. Songs of praise the an - gels sang, Heaven with hal - le - lu - jahs rang, When Je - ho - vah's

work be - gun, When he spake, and it was done. 2. Songs of praise a - woke the morn,

work be - gun, When he spake, and it was done. 2. Songs of praise a - woke the morn,

When the Prince of Peace was born; Songs of praise a - rose, when he, Cap - tive led cap-

When the Prince of Peace was born; Songs of praise a - rose, when he, Cap - tive led cap-

tiv - i - ty. 3. Heaven and earth must pass a - way— Songs of praise shall crown that day;

tiv - i - ty. 3. Heaven and earth must pass a - way— Songs of praise shall crown that day;

SONGS OF PRAISE. Continued.

God will make new heavens and earth—Songs of praise shall hail their birth. 4. And shall man a-

God will make new heavens and earth—Songs of praise shall hail their birth. 4. And shall man a-

lone be dumb, Till that glo - rious king - dom come? No; the Church de - lights to raise

lone be dumb, Till that glo - rious king - dom come? No; the Church de - lights to raise

Play eight bars interlude.

Psalms and hymns and songs of praise. 5. Saints be - low, with heart and voice, Still in

Psalms and hymns and songs of praise. 5. Saints be - low, with heart and voice, Still in

songs of praise re - joice; Learning here, by faith and love, Songs of

songs of praise re - joice; Learn - ing here, by faith and love, Songs of

Ped.

SONGS OF PRAISE. Concluded.

praise to sing a-bove. 6. Borne up-on their lat-est breath Songs of praise shall conquer death;

praise to sing a-bove. 6. Borne up-on their lat-est breath Songs of praise shall conquer death;

Then, a-mid e-ter-nal joy, Songs of praise their powers em-ploy. Borne up-on their

Then, a-mid e-ter-nal joy, Songs of praise their powers em-ploy. Borne up-on their

lat-est breath Songs of praise shall con-quer death; Then, a-mid e-ter-nal joy,

lat-est breath Songs of praise shall con-quer death; Then, a-mid e-ter-nal joy,

Then, a-mid e-ternal joy, Songs of praise their powers employ, Songs of praise their powers employ.

ritard.

Then, a-mid e-ternal joy, Songs of praise their powers employ, Songs of praise their powers employ.

Hymn 133. **PRAISE TO THEE.** 8s & 7s. J. P. H.

1. Praise to thee, thou great Cre - a - tor! Praise to thee from ev - ery tongue;

1. Praise to thee, thou great Cre - a - tor! Praise to thee from ev - ery tongue;

Join, my soul, with ev - ery crea - ture, Join the u - ni - ver - sal song.

Join, my soul, with ev - ery crea - ture, Join the u - ni - ver - sal song.

SOLO. SOPRANO.

2. Fa - ther! source..... of all com - pas - sion! Pure, un - bound - ed grace is thine:

Hail the God........ of our sal - va - tion, Praise him for...... his love di - vine!

rit.

cres.

PRAISE TO THEE. Continued.

3. For ten thou-sand bless-ings giv - en, For the hope of fu - ture joy,

3. For ten thou - sand bless-ings giv - en, For the hope of fu - ture joy,

Sound his praise through earth and heav - en, Sound Je - ho - vah's praise on high!

Sound his praise through earth and heav - en, Sound Je - ho - vah's praise on high!

DUET. TENOR & BASS.

4. Praise to God,...... the great Cre - a - tor, Fa - ther, Son,...... and Ho - ly Ghost;

4. Praise to God,...... the great Cre - a - tor, Fa - ther, Son,...... and Ho - ly Ghost;

Praise him ev - ery liv - ing crea - ture, Earth and heaven's u - nit - ed host.

Praise him ev - ery liv - ing crea - ture, Earth and heaven's u - nit - ed host.

PRAISE TO THEE. Concluded.

5. Joy - ful - ly.... on earth a - dore him, Till in heaven our song we raise;

ff sempre.

5. Joy - ful - ly.... on earth a - dore him, Till in heaven our song we raise;

Then en - rapt - ured fall be - fore him, Lost in won - der, love, and praise!

rit.

Then en - rapt - ured fall be - fore him, Lost in won - der, love, and praise!

Hymn 142. **THOU WHO ART ENTHRONED. 7s.** J. P. H.

Quartet. Allegro moderato.

1. Thou who art en - throned a - bove, Thou by whom we live and move!

f

1. Thou who art en - throned a - bove, Thou by whom we live and move!

Oh, how sweet, with joy - ful tongue, To re - sound thy praise in song!

Oh, how sweet, with joy - ful tongue, To re - sound thy praise in song!

THOU WHO ART ENTHRONED. Continued.

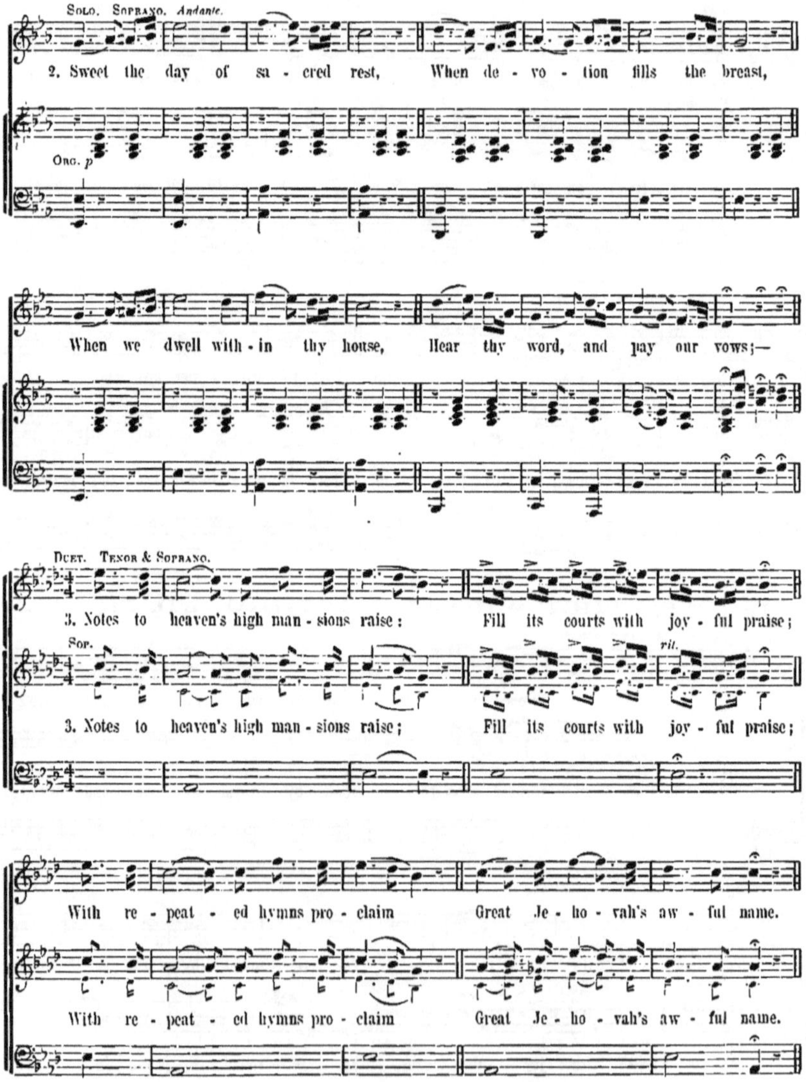

THOU WHO ART ENTHRONED. Concluded.

Quartet. *Allegro moderato.*

4. From thy works our joys a - rise, O thou on - ly good and wise!

4. From thy works our joys a - rise, O thou on - ly good and wise!

Who thy won - ders can de - clare? How pro - found thy coun - sels are!

ritard.

Who thy won - ders can de - clare? How pro - found thy coun - sels are!

Chorus.

5. Warm our hearts with sa - cred fire; Grate - ful fer - vors still in - spire;

ff

5. Warm our hearts with sa - cred fire; Grate - ful fer - vors still in - spire;

Ped.

All..... our powers, with all.... their might, Ev - er in...... thy praise u - nite.

All..... our powers, with all..... their might, Ev - er in...... thy praise u - nite.

184

LORD, THY GLORY FILLS THE HEAVEN.

Hymn 265.

L. H. SOUTHARD, by permission.

1. Lord,.... thy glo - - ry fills the heav - en;
2. Ev - - er thus in God's high prais - es,
3. Lord,.... thy glo - - ry fills the heav - en;

Earth is with...... its full - - ness stored:
Breth - - ren. let....... our tongues u - nite,
Earth is with...... its full - - ness stored;

Un - to thee.... be glo - ry giv - en, Ho - ly, ho - ly,
While our thoughts his greatness rais - es, And our love his
Un - to thee.... be glo - ry giv - en, Ho - ly, ho - ly,

ho - ly Lord!
gifts.... ex - cite;
ho - ly Lord!
Heav'n is still.... with an - thems
With his ser - aph train...... be -
Thus thy glo - rious name,...... con -
ring - ing; Earth takes up the an - gels' cry.
fore him, With his ho - ly church be - low,
fess - ing, We a - dopt the an - gels' cry,

Ho - ly, ho - ly,   ho - ly,   sing - ing,   Lord   of   hosts,   thou
Thus   u - nite we   to   a - dore him,   Bid   we   thus   our
Ho - ly, ho - ly,   ho - ly,   bless - ing,   Thee   the   Lord,   our

Lord   most   high.
an - them   flow.
God   most   high!

Ho - ly,   ho - ly,   ho - ly,
Thus   u - nite   we   to   a -

Ho - ly,   ho - ly,   ho - ly.

LORD, THY GLORY. Concluded.

First system (vocal text):

Lord.................... of hosts,.... thou Lord most high,
Bid.................... we thus.... our an - them flow,
Thee,................... the Lord.... our God most high,

sing - ing, Lord.... of hosts, thou Lord.... most high,
dore him, Bid..... we thus our an - them flow,

bless - ing Thee,.... the Lord our God.... most high,

Second system (vocal text):

Lord of hosts, thou Lord most high,
Bid we thus our an - them flow,
Thee, the Lord our God most high.

A - - men.

Lord of hosts, thou Lord most high.
Bid we thus our an - them flow,

A - - men.

Thee, the Lord our God most high.

A - - men.

D. C. dal 𝄋 | Coda for last verse.

mf

f adagio.

OH, HOW LOVELY IS ZION.

Adapted from the "Lyra Catholica," by permission.

Andante moderato.

SOLO. SOPRANO.

Oh,.... how love - ly, love - - ly is

_mf_ _p_

Zi - on, Zi - - on, cit - y, Zi - on, cit - y of our God,... our

God; Joy and peace, joy and peace shall dwell in thee, shall dwell in thee, in thee, *ad lib.*

Joy..... and peace shall dwell in thee.

Solo. Contralto.

Oh,.... how love-ly, how love-ly is Zi - on, Oh, how

love - ly is Zi - on, cit - y of our God; Joy and peace shall dwell in thee, Joy and

peace shall.. dwell in thee.

OH, HOW LOVELY IS ZION. Continued.

Oh, how love-ly, how love-ly is

Oh, how love-ly, love-ly is

Oh, how love-ly, how love-ly is

Zi - on, Zi - on, cit - - - y of our God, Joy and peace shall dwell in thee,

Zi - on, Zi - on, cit - - - y of our God, Joy and peace shall dwell in thee,

Zi - on, Zi - on, cit - - - y of our God. Shall .... dwell in thee,

OH, HOW LOVELY IS ZION. Concluded.

Shall dwell, shall dwell in thee, Joy and peace shall dwell in thee, shall dwell in

Shall dwell, shall dwell in thee, Joy and peace shall dwell in thee, shall dwell in

Shall dwell, shall dwell in thee. Joy and peace shall dwell in thee, shall dwell in

thee, Joy and peace shall dwell in thee, Joy and peace shall dwell in thee.

thee, Joy and peace shall dwell in thee, Joy and peace shall dwell in thee.

thee, Joy and peace shall dwell in thee, Joy and peace shall dwell in thee.

I WILL EXTOL THEE.

MOZART.

Adapted from the " Lyra Catholica," by permission.

TRIO.—SOPRANO, CONTRALTO & BASS.

Andantino.

SOPRANO.

I will ex - tol thee, my God, O king; And I will bless thy name for -

CONTRALTO.

I will ex - tol thee, my God, O king; And I will bless thy name for -

ev - er; I will ex - tol thee, and I will bless thee; I will

ev - er; I will ex - tol thee, and I will bless thee; I will

praise thy name for - ev - er, thy name for - ev - er and ev - er.
praise thy name for - ev - er, thy name for - ev - er and ev - er.
Ev - ery day I will bless thee, and I will praise thy name for - ev - er and
Ev - ery day I will bless thee, and I will praise thy name for - ev - er and
Ped.
pp
Trio. Soprano.
Contralto.
ev - er. I will ex - tol thee, my God, O
Bass.
ev - er. I will ex - tol thee, my God, O
pp
mp
Ped.

I WILL EXTOL THEE. Concluded.

king;   And I will bless thy name for - ev - er, thy name for-

king; And I will bless,   will bless thy name for - ev - er, thy name for-

I will bless thee.

ev - er and ev - er.   Ev - ery day I will bless........... thee.

ev - er and ev - er.   I will bless thee.

and I will

and I will praise thy name for - ev - er.   A - - men.   A - - men.

for - ev - er,   A - - men.   A - - men.

dim. al fine.   *lento.*   *perdendosi.*

Hymn 116. **HOLY, HOLY, HOLY LORD.** 7s.   Abt.

Ho-ly, ho-ly, ho-ly Lord God of Hosts! when heav'n and earth, Out of dark - ness, at thy

Ho-ly, ho-ly, ho-ly Lord God of Hosts! when heav'n and earth, Out of darkness, at thy

Out of

word.... Is-sued in-to glo-rious birth, All thy work be-fore thee stood, And thine

word.... Is-sued in-to glo-rious birth, All thy work be-fore thee stood, And thine

darkness at thy word

eye be-held them good, Ho - ly, ho - ly, ho - ly Lord! While they

eye be-held them good, While they sung with sweet ac-cord. Ho-ly, ho-ly, ho-ly Lord!..........

Solo. Bass.

Ho - ly, ho - ly, ho - ly Lord! While they

Ho - ly

sung with sweet ac - cord, Ho-ly, ho-ly, ho-ly Lord! Ho - ly Lord!

sung with sweet ac - cord, Ho - ly Lord! Ho-ly, ho-ly, ho-ly Lord!

Solo. Bass.

sung with sweet ac - c , Ho - ly Lord! ho - ly, Lord!

CAST THY BURDEN ON THE LORD.

MERCADANTE.

Cast thy bur-den on the Lord, And he shall, he shall sus-tain thee,

Cast thy bur-den on the Lord,

Cast thy bur-den on the Lord,

He will not suf-fer thee to fall, He...... will not suf-fer thee......

He will not suf-fer thee to fall,

He will not suf-fer thee to fall,

to fall, Cast thy bur - den on the
Cast thy bur-den,
Cast thy bur-den on the Lord,....
mf cres.
f

Lord, And he shall sus-tain thee, He shall sus-tain thee, He
on the Lord, He
on the Lord,.... He
ff
f

CAST THY BURDEN. Continued.

shall sustain, sus-tain thee, Cast thy bur - den

shall sustain, sus-tain thee, Cast thy

shall sus-tain thee, Cast thy bur - den, Cast thy bur - den

ou the Lord, And he shall sus-tain thee, He shall sus-

bur-den on the Lord,

on the Lord,....

f cres.

CAST THY BURDEN. Concluded.

tain   thee,   He   shall sus - tain   thee, The Lord   shall sus - tain   thee,   The Lord

He   shall sns - tain   thee,   shall sns - tain   thee,

He   shall sus - tain   thee,   shall sus - tain   thee,

shall sus - tain   thee,   up - on   the Lord.

shall sus - tain   thee,   up - on   the Lord.

shall sus - tain   thee,   Cast thy bur - den   on   the   Lord.................

"COME UNTO ME, ALL YE THAT LABOR."

Largo. 50. = ♩.   Haydn.

Sw. 2 Diaps.

Ch. Dulciana.

Solo. Soprano.

Come un - to me,   all   ye............. that

la - bor.   And............. ....   are hea - vy

la - den,   And   I   will give you rest,...... and   I   will give   you

COME UNTO ME. Continued.

COME UNTO ME. Continued.

yoke up - on you, And learn of me, For I am meek and

yoke up - on you, And learn of me, For I am meek and

yoke up - on you, Aud learn of me. For I am meek and

low - ly in heart, And ye shall find rest un - to, un -

low - ly iu heart. And ye shall...... find rest......... un -

low - ly iu heart, And ye shall find rest un - to, un -

-to your souls, And ye shall, shall find rest un - to..... your souls.
-to your souls, And ye shall, shall find rest un - to..... your souls,
-to your souls, And ye shall, shall find rest un - to..... your souls.
Gt. Diaps. & Principal.
f
p
Tutti. pp
For, my yoke is ea - sy, is
Tutti. pp
For, my yoke is ea - sy, is
Tutti. pp
For, my yoke is ea - sy, And my bur - - den is
Tutti. pp
Sw. Stop Diap. only.
pp
Double Diap. alone.
8

COME UNTO ME. Concluded.

light, is ea - sy, and my bur - den is light, is light.

light, is ea - sy, and my bur - den is light, is light.

light, For my yoke..... is ea - sy, and my bur - - den is light, is light.

pp

"THOUGH SORROWS RISE."

Hymn 788.

F. Butler. From "Lyra Catholica," by permission

1. Though sor - rows rise and dan - gers roll, In waves of darkness o'er my soul;

cres.

1. Though sor - rows rise and dan - gers roll, In waves of darkness o'er my soul;

Though friends are false, and love de - cays, And few and e - vil are my days;

Though friends are false, and love de - cays, And few and e - vil are my days;

THOUGH SORROWS RISE. Continued.

Though conscience, fierc - est of my foes, Swells with re - membered guilt my woes;

p

Though conscience, fierc - est of my foes, Swells with re - membered guilt my woes;

Yet ev'n in na - ture's ut - most ill, I love thee, Lord! I love thee still!

cres.   *f*   *ritard.*   *f a tempo.*

Org.

Yet ev'n in na - ture's ut - most ill, I love thee, Lord! I love thee still!

2. Though Si - nai's curse, in thun - der dread, Peals o'er mine un - pro - tect - ed head,

f

2. Though Si - nai's curse, in thun - der dread, Peals o'er mine un - pro - tect - ed head,

And memory points, with bus - y pain, To grace and mer - cy given in vain;

p   *p*

And memory points, with bus - y pain, To grace and mer - cy given in vain;

THOUGH SORROWS RISE. Continued.

p Solo Tenor.

Till na - ture, shrink-ing in the strife,

Solo Soprano. *ad lib.*

Till na - ture, shrink-ing in the strife, Would fly to hell to

Would fly to hell to 'scape from life;

cres.

Would fly to hell to 'scape from life; I

'scape from life; Though ev - ery thought has power to kill, I

love thee, Lord! I love thee still.

Org.

love thee, Lord! I love thee still.

3. Oh, by the pangs thy - self hast borne, The ruf - fians blow the ty - rant's scorn,

p

3. Oh, by the pangs thy - self hast borne, The ruf - fians blow the ty - rant's scorn,

THOUGH SORROWS RISE. Concluded.

By Si - nai's curse, whose dread - ful doom Was bur - ied in thy guilt - less tomb;

By these my pangs, whose heal - ing smart Thy grace hath plant - ed in my heart—

I know, I feel thy boun-teous will, Thou lov'st me, Lord! thou lov'st me still, Thou lov'st me.

Lord, thou lov'st me still, Thou lov'st me, Lord, thou lov'st me still.

SENTENCE. "I will arise." J. P. H.

Soprano Solo. *Larghetto.*

I will a - rise, I will a - rise and go to my Fa - ther,

mp

And will say un - to him, Fa - - ther, Fa - - ther,

pp *f* *pp* *rit.*

I have sin-ned, I have sin - ned, Against Heav'n and be - fore,... thee...

f *pp* *ff* *pp*

And am no more wor-thy, And am no more wor-thy to be call - ed thy

pp *rit.*

I WILL ARISE. Concluded.

Fa - ther, I have sin - ned, Fa - ther, I have sin - ned against Heaven and be - fore.... thee..... And am no more wor - thy to be call - ed thy Son......

SENTENCE. The Sacrifices of God. J. P. H.

The Sac - ri - fi - ces of God are a bro - ken spir - it. A broken and a con - trite heart, O God thou wilt not de - spise, wilt not de - spise...

GLORIA IN EXCELSIS.

Jno. Underner

1. Glory be to | God on | high; | And on earth | peace, good | will to-wards | men.

1. Glory be to | God on | high; | And on earth | peace, good | will to-wards | men.

2. We praise thee, we bless thee, we | worship | thee, | We glorify thee, we give thanks to | thee for | thy great | glory:

2. We praise thee, we bless thee, we | worship | thee, | We glorify thee, we give thanks to | thee for | thy great | glory;

3. O Lord God, | heaven-ly | King, | God the | Father Al - | mighty. 4. O Lord, the only begotten Son, |

3. O Lord God, | heaven-ly | King, | God the | Father Al - | mighty. 4. O Lord, the only begotten Son, |

Je - sus | Christ; | O Lord God, Lamb of | God, Son | of the | Father.

Je - sus | Christ; | O Lord God, Lamb of | God, Son | of the | Father.

Lento.

5. That takest away the | sins of the | world, | have | mer - cy up - | on us.
pp   *cres - - - - - cen - - - - - do.*

6. Thou that takest away the | sins of the | world, | have | mer - cy up - | on us,
7. Thou that takest away the | sins of the | world, | re - - | ceive our — | prayer.

8. Thou that sittest at the right hand of | God the | Father, | have | mer - cy up - |
ff   *pp*

8. Thou that sittest at the right hand of | God the | Father, | have | mer - cy up - |

on - | us. ‖ 9. For thou only | art.... | holy; | thou | on - ly | art the | Lord; ‖
ff

on - | us. ‖ 9. For thou only | art ... | holy; | thou | on - ly | art the | Lord; ‖

10. Thou only, O Christ, with the | Ho - ly | Ghost, | art most high in the | glory of | God the | Father. ‖ A - - | men. ‖
                     pp

10. Thou only, O Christ, with the | Ho - ly | Ghost, | art most high in the | glory of | God the | Father. ‖ A - - | men. ‖

"COME UNTO ME ALL YE THAT LABOR."

LEPREVOST.

DUET FOR SOPRANO AND CONTRALTO.

Adapted from "Lyra Catholica," by permission.

Andante sostenuto.

SOPRANO.

Come un - to me...... all ye.... that la - bor and are heavy la - den, and

CONTRALTO.

I will give, and I will give you rest,.... Come un - to me...... all ye.... that la - bor and are heav - y lad - en, And I will give, And

ye.... that la - bor and are heav - y lad - en, And I will give, And

I will give you rest.

I will give you rest.

and learn...... of.... me,....

Take my yoke...... up - on you, For

For   I am meek and low - ly in

I am meek and low - ly in heart,....

heart,   And ye shall find rest un - to   your souls.

And ye shall find rest un - to   your souls.

For my yoke is ea - sy, and my bur - den is light,   For my yoke is

For my yoke is ea - sy, and my bur - den is light,   For my yoke is

cres.

p
ea - sy, and my bur - den is light. For my yoke is
p
ea - sy, and my bur - den is light, For my yoke is
p
ea - sy, and my bur - den is light, For my yoke is ea - sy, and my
p
ea - sy, and my bur - den is light, For my yoke is ea - sy, and my
retard.
bur - den is light.
bur - den is light.

Hymn 1087.   **"ONLY THEE."**   Lepaevost.

Soprano Solo and Quartet.   Adapted from "Lyra Catholica," by permission.

Andante Sostenuto.

Bless - ed Sav - iour!

thee   I   love,........   All   my oth - er   joys   a - bove, All my

oth - er   joys   a - bove;

ritard.

Sop. Solo.

All my hopes in thee a - bide,.... Thou my hope, and naught be-

Soprano.

Contralto.

All my hopes in thee a - bide,.... Thou my hope, and

Tenor.

All my hopes in thee a - bide,.... Thou my hope, and

Bass.

side: All my hopes...... in thee abide, Thou my hope, and naught be -

naught beside: All my hopes ..... in thee abide, Thou my hope, and naught be -

naught beside: All my hopes...... in thee abide, Thou my hope, and naught be -

cres. *f*

side : Ev - er let........ my glo - ry be, Ev - er let my glo - ry

side, naught beside : Ev - er let my glo - ry be, let my glo - ry

side, naught beside : Ev - er let my glo - ry be, let my glo - ry

p

be, On - ly thee,...... on - ly thee. On - ly thee, on - ly

be, thee, on - ly

be, thee, on - ly

p *f*

thee.

thee.

thee.

thee.

p

rallent.

Ev - er let my glo - ry be, On - ly,

Ev - er let my glo - ry be, On - ly,

Ev - er let my glo - ry be, On - ly,

"ONLY THEE." Concluded.

on - ly, on - ly thee,.... Ev - er let my glo - ry be   On - ly thee,

on - ly   thee, Ev - er let my glo - ry   be,   On - ly   thee.

on - ly   thee, Ev - er let my glo - ry   be,   On - ly   thee,

Ev - er let my glo-ry be,   On -   ly   thee.

Ev - er let my glo-ry be,   On -   ly   thee.

Ev - er let my glo-ry be,   On -   ly   thee.

slentando. f pp

INDEX OF FIRST LINES.

INDEX OF TUNES.

INDEX OF METRES.

MISCELLANEOUS.